MEMOIRS/JOURNEY OF A PUBLIC HEALTH EDUCATOR

A Journey through State Health Departments, Community Health Centers and Non-profit Organizations Utilizing Health Education Concepts and Exploring Health and Well-being among the Uninsured Population in the United States

2nd Edition – March 2024

DAVE BRANGAN, MS, CHES
HEALTH EDUCATION CONSULTANTS, INC.
PO Box 308, Irmo, South Carolina 29063

The Mission of Health Education Consultants is to alleviate the suffering and prevent or delay the onset of chronic diseases such as obesity, diabetes, hypertension, heart disease among medically underserved and uninsured populations in South Carolina through health education, wellness, and changes in lifestyle.

June 1, 2024

TABLE OF CONTENTS

Introduction..4

Chapter One – Prequel – US Army Vietnam 6

Chapter Two – West Virginia – The Early Years....................................... 12

Chapter Three – Graduate School at West Virginia University.................…..........19

Chapter Four – Transition from Graduate School to Health Professional..........................23

Chapter Five – Developing the AIDS Program for the State of West Virginia.....................25

Chapter Six – Using Health Education Skills Learned in Grad School..............................28

Chapter Seven – AIDS Education for the Public…...…..30

Chapter Eight – HIV/AIDS Ancillary Programs – Strange Bedfellows...............................32

Chapter 9 – Off to the South Carolina Department of Health.......................................36

Chapter 10 – The Ryan White AIDS Clinic…...…......43

Chapter 11 – Health Promotion at Edisto Health District….............................….......54

Chapter 12 – Maternal and Child Health at the Edisto Health District.............................56

Chapter 13 – Family Health Center, Inc …...…62

Chapter 14 – Interim Jobs – Blue Cross Blue Shield and Health and Human Services….........72

Chapter 15 – Brief Returns to Department of Health and Family Health Center, Inc..............74

Chapter 16 – Hope Health, Inc…...….........76

Chapter 17 – The Wonderful World of Non-Profits…...78

Chapter 18 – Columbia Free Medical Clinic…..…..........86

Chapter 19 – Newberry Free Medical Clinic….......................................…..........93

Chapter 20 – Good Samaritan Clinics ….......................................…....…..........101

Chapter 21 – Culture and Public Health Organizations…..........................…......…....105

Epilog…...…. ….110

Appendix One – Health Education Consultants Response to Covid19............................114
Appendix Two - Patient Testimonies ………………………………………………….....117
Appendix Three – Health Education Consultants Inc. Documents ……………………......129
Appendix Four – Healthcare Reform Articles …………………………………………..........131
Appendix Five - For the Academic (Health Statistics) ……………………………………..158
Contact Information…………………………………………………………………..……....164

Introduction

The profession, Public Health Education, has its origins in the late 1970's and early 1980's when a group of health professionals and educators met in New York City to form the National Commission for Health Education Credentialing. The goals were many, though foremost was to establish Health Education as a profession with a Bachelor's, Master's, and doctorate degrees. The commission spent several years defining the roles and delineations for health educators in public health, school health, corporate wellness programs and community health. The committee worked hard to write a document called the "Roles and Delineations for Health Educators" and developed a national qualifying exam to award the CHES (Certified Health Education Specialist) certificate and later a master's Certified Health Education Specialist as a credential next to their name, not unlike RN, M.D., and other professional designations. The profession has come a long way since those early years.

This book is about one man's journey as a Public Health Educator from 1986 to 2024, some 37 years in all. The journey will begin with the early days of the AIDS epidemic in the 1980's and 90's until the closing days of the COVID 19 epidemic in 2022. In addition, there will be the life experiences of a professional health educator (myself). Along the way, we will explore the various health care systems in the United States, the patients who use the health care systems and the role of health education and prevention. Therefore, there will be some advice for future health educators when developing health education programs for the major chronic diseases.

It should be noted that the beginning of my career as a professional Health Educator begins with the first two chapters which are precursors related to the profession: (1) my experiences in the US Army with the Medical Service Corp (MSC) during the Vietnam War (1967) and (2) five years working at the West Virginia University Hospital (1979 – 1984). These experiences led me to choose Public Health Education as a career. Also, I will be writing about "Stories from the Field" which I think you will find quite interesting with some being facetious and some being sad. Either way, it will be quite a journey!

The first thing a publisher asks the writer of a book is: who is the intended audience? The answer is twofold: (1) the public, however more specifically those who care about the health and well-being of those without healthcare insurance and (2) practicing public health professionals and students of public health, especially health education practitioners.

For those interested, In the appendix, I have included several articles I wrote for the Orangeburg, SC newspaper, "The Times and Democrat" in 2010/11 concerning healthcare reform. However, this book is not necessarily about healthcare reform, just my journey through the healthcare system in the United States and the plight of the uninsured patient.

This second edition will include additional stories from the field, observations made during my journey through the public health clinics, and an update on the Affordable Care Act also known as Obamacare.

Chapter One –

Prequel -US Army Vietnam

In June of 1966, I enlisted in the US Army at Fort Jackson, South Carolina, just as the Vietnam War was heating up. I was 22 years old at the time and had completed two years of college. My major at West Virginia University was journalism and I had a curiosity about wars and why one human being would kill another human being over some political dispute. To make a long story short, I completed basic training and advanced training for a clerical/administrative job specialty. I arrived in Vietnam in November 1966 ready for my first assignment at the 55th Medical Group in QuiNhon, along the Vietnam coast. This was Headquarters for the 55th Medical Group of surgical hospitals in the area: the 85 Evacuation and 67th Evacuation Hospitals. This was my first exposure to the medical field as Medevac helicopters with wounded soldiers flew in regularly as we slept in our tents at night. The 85th Evacuation Hospital was a Quonset hut, a metal dome shaped structure with cement floors and metal beds. As the wounded soldiers came into the hospital, I noticed that some of the wounded were from the North Vietnamese Army. One of my job responsibilities at the 55th Medical Group was to catalog and keep track of the enemy soldiers, including the Viet Cong (enemy soldiers from South Vietnam), who were admitted to the 85th Evacuation Hospital. They were interrogated by the Army's military intelligence officers as to their status. Some were innocent farmers who happened to be caught in a firefight. I would walk through the hospital wards and see wounded US Army soldiers lying in bed and the next bed over, was a wounded enemy soldier. It was an interesting juxtaposition so to speak. In a strange way, this was my introduction to public health. In other words, every soldier, whether American, North Vietnamese, or Vietnamese civilian, was given medical treatment by US Army doctors, nurses, and staff. I was merely the administrative person. Another startling moment was when I met a North Vietnamese Army (NVA) soldier who was a medic (he wore a red cross on his sleeve) and was working in the 85th Evacuation hospital helping US Army doctors and nurses care for patients. I had a brief chat with him (the hospital staff called him Mikey), however I don't remember the content of that conversation as it was short, and I was busy with my clerical duties. I do remember looking at him straight in the eye with him looking at me straight in the eye and both of us wondering what we were doing here in the middle of a war, especially at such a young age. There was an emotional exchange there which is difficult to describe. As I performed my job in the hospital, categorizing the Vietnamese patients, I often wondered what happened to them after they recovered from their wounds. Some Vietnamese were categorized by the US Army intelligence officer as "detainees" in other words it was uncertain if they were North Vietnamese soldiers, Viet Cong, South Vietnamese soldiers, or innocent bystanders (civilians). When they came into the hospital by helicopter or ground ambulance, their wounds were often so severe that their clothing or uniforms were torn apart, thus impossible to identify their status. When I asked the interrogating officer what would happen to the detainees and other enemy soldiers who were patients, he simply said they were turned over to the South Vietnam government for further interrogation and possible imprisonment. At age 22, all of this was rather a life-changing experience. Prior to Vietnam, all I knew were sports, girls, part time jobs and having a good time. I had to grow up, right away!

While working at 55th Medical Group headquarters, which was across the "street" from the 85th Evacuation Hospital, I watched the Army doctors and nurses heroically treating all patients coming in by helicopter 24 hours per day. They were all courageous and very mission oriented.

After several months in QuiNohn, I was transferred to the 142nd Medical Detachment, in Phu Thanh, some 10 miles from QuiNohn. The 142nd was a dispensary, like Urgent Care in the Unites States today. I was the company clerk, like Radar on MASH. It was a unique position as I could see everything about our unit operations, personnel coming and going, ordering supplies, and assisting the medics when treating the patients. The 142nd Medical Detachment was staffed by a couple of physicians, a dentist, a lab technician, a pharmacist and three medics. There was an LPN (licensed practical nurse) equivalent position there also. We had "sick call" every morning for the Army soldiers who were stationed nearby. These were supply units, transportation, mess hall/cooks, and finance units. I helped with sick calls and maintained medical records, and as company clerk, I maintained personnel records and ordered medical supplies. After sick call for the Americans, there was "sick call" for the Vietnamese who lived in the area. They all lined up outside the dispensary, however we didn't have any interpreters or even medical records for the Vietnamese. We did the best we could. Our dispensary was a walk-in emergency room as well. We received injuries from local Vietnamese civilians for vehicle accidents and some casualties from the war. There was a shortage of medics, so I learned how to treat injuries as a medic and even did some suturing for skin lacerations. Therefore, I was the Company Clerk, maintained medical records, helped organize daily sick call for military personnel and Vietnamese and even helped with the delivery of medical care. Added to all these responsibilities was being a US Army soldier carrying AR-15 rifle, pulling guard duty and being on the constant guard or lookout for the enemy which looked like the civilian population around the dispensary. The Viet Cong blended in with the local South Vietnamese population. All of this at age 22.

I share this prequel because you will see the connection from my experiences in medical hospitals and dispensaries in Vietnam to The Free Medical Clinics in South Carolina today. I know that sounds like quite a leap, however I will connect the dots for you! Just to continue the prequel a little further, I returned to West Virginia University after my three years in the military, used the GI Bill, and earned my bachelor's and master's Degrees (See Chapter Two of prequel.) As I worked my way through the rest of my academic career, I joined the Army Reserves in Morgantown and Fairmont, West Virginia. The Fairmont Reserve unit was the 445th Medical Company (Clearing) which was like a MASH unit where casualties (simulated) would come in, receive medical treatment, and then be evacuated to a permanent treatment facility like a hospital. I supervised the Admissions and Dispositions section, a unique position as I could see all the "action" from beginning to end as the simulated patients made their way through the facility (our unit). In addition to the simulated action, there was a "real" sick call each day for our unit and other units operating in the field. This went on for several years with summer camps at Fort Bragg, North Carolina, Fort Meade, Maryland, Fort Gordon, Georgia and Fort AP Hill, Virginia.

My last Army Reserve assignment was at Fort Jackson, SC with the 3270th Army Hospital at Moncrief Army Hospital where I managed the Patient Administration section and participated in Desert Storm in 1991. Unbeknownst to myself, I wondered if God was looking out for me back then, even when I was in Vietnam and continuing through the Army Reserves and into Public Health. Finally, after 20 years in the Army combining 3 ½ years active duty and 17 years Reserves, I qualified for full retirement benefits including a monthly retirement paycheck and medical coverage with Tricare. God was indeed looking out for me again!

Stories from the Field – Vietnam - 1967

Vietnamese girl shot in the back and killed after stealing lumber from Army compound - 1967

When you think of a war, one thinks of battlefield casualties, however there are many civilian casualties as well. There was one instance while stationed at the 142nd Medical Detachment when we received a call regarding a Vietnamese girl who was shot in the back when stealing lumber from a military installation nearby. We had a ground ambulance at our disposal, and we were all set to make the emergency run when we were told not to bother going to the scene because she was dead, and they would transport the body to the 85th Evacuation hospital morgue. I often wondered about her, her age, why she was stealing lumber, who shot her, and what her family would think and feel about the entire incident.

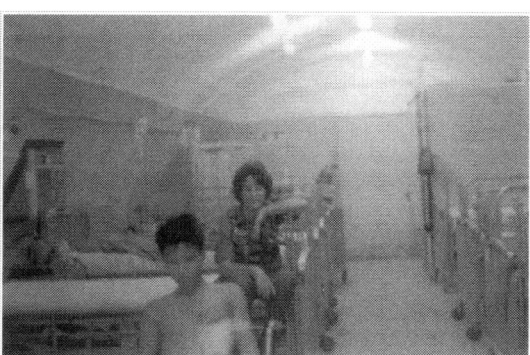

US Army Nurse at the 85th Evacuation Hospital, QuiNohn, Vietnam 1966.

Trauma along the roadside in Phu Thanh, South Vietnam - 1967

PhuThanh was a small town with dirt roads and houses made of tin and plywood. There was the constant smell of wood burning, food cooking, fish frying, rice, and other Vietnamese staples. For some reason, many of these houses or huts were right along the dirt roadside. There was an instance where a truck ran over a family cooking a meal which was a mile or two from our 142nd dispensary. It was at lunchtime and there was only me and one other medic in the building. A Vietnamese man ran into the dispensary crying and handed me his baby not even 6 months old. The baby was apparently dead and covered in dirt, having been run over by the vehicle. The baby wasn't breathing and there was dirt in his/her mouth. I cleared the airway the best I could and attempted CPR, but it was no use. I gave the baby to the other medic and told him I was going to the mess hall to get our two doctors and other dispensary staff who were at lunch. On the way out, a young girl was walking in the dispensary with her arm severed above the elbow and nothing but a bone protruding from her upper arm. She was in shock and there was no bleeding, apparently the trauma to the arm was so severe that it stopped bleeding. I hopped in the jeep and went full speed up the road to the mess hall and found our two doctors and told them about the accident and civilian casualties. I think I was not coherent when telling them I was so terrified by the trauma I just witnessed. They got the message and returned to the dispensary as fast as they could. There were a few more casualties from this "accident" however they were not as severe as the first two walk-ins. The rest of the medics took over and evacuated the injured to the 85th Evacuation Hospital. I will never forget the expressions on the face of the father carrying his dead baby in his arms and handing the baby over to me to save the baby's life. And the expression on the young girl's face when she walked in the dispensary with a bone protruding out from her right upper arm.

Chapter Two –

The West Virginia Years

After being discharged from the Army in 1969, I returned to West Virginia University in Morgantown, West Virginia. I had two years of college under my belt, and I needed two more for my bachelor's degree. I remember my father telling me he would pay for the first two years of college, however after that, I was on my own! In other words, I had to pay my own way through the rest of college not to mention paying for an apartment and feeding myself. Thinking back, that is probably one of the best things he did for me as I had to take responsibility for myself and be independent. Thankfully, I had the GI Bill from my three years in the Army so all I had to do was find a part-time job to pay for an apartment and food. I couldn't be particular about what kind of job if there was a paycheck!

West Virginia University had a huge Medical Center as it was a teaching hospital complete with major medical surgeries and allied health schools. Since I was in the health services field in the Army, I thought I would apply for a job at the Medical Center. The only job opening they had at the time was in food service, which was basically working in the kitchen, preparing food trays, and delivering them to patients on a mobile cart, bringing the cart up the elevators and to the patient's rooms; then retrieving the trays later after the patients completed their meal. This was not a glamorous job; however, it was a steady paycheck. I was hoping to get a free meal from time to time, however this never happened! I had to work full time to pay my bills which meant I could attend West Virginia University only part-time. Therefore, it took me longer to get my degree finally in 1974.

Since it was taking me so long to get through undergraduate school going part-time, I thought I would apply for different positions within the West Virginia University Hospital. I applied for a job as an orderly which is known as a nurse technician today! I think the stereotype for the orderly was getting bedpans for patients in the middle of the night, which isn't too far from the truth! I had lots of patient interactions and spent a lot of time listening to patient's stories and medical complaints. At the same time, I enjoyed working with the doctors, nurses, X-Ray technicians and the hospital environment in general. In a way, I was working my way through college and enjoying it. However, after a year or two of giving baths to patients and bringing bedpans to them in the middle of the night, I was ready for a change, so I applied for a position in the medical records section of the hospital. This was back in the day before electronic medical records, so everything was on paper and had to be filed and retrieved manually. When I applied for the medical records position, I mentioned to the interviewer that I maintained medical records in the Army while I was in Vietnam, at the 142nd Medical Dispensary. The interviewer was so impressed he hired me on the spot! This was another fun job while I was attending West Virginia University taking courses in my major, Political Science, on a part-time basis. I say it was a fun job because I was learning my way around the hospital emergency room, outpatient clinics, operating room, administration and so forth. Most of the physicians on staff had offices within the building with medical secretaries who were always calling and looking for medical records for certain patients. The medical center was eight stories high, and the medical records could be anywhere in the building! The medical records department had a sign-out card like a library card (back in the day) where one would have to trace all the signatures and departments as to who checked out the medical record and the checkout date! While this was another "fun" job, I was ready to move on after a year or two while continuing my studies part time. There was a job opening in the Emergency Department as an admissions clerk. Again, drawing on my military experience in Vietnam, I thought I would be a good fit for this position and so I was hired virtually on the spot again. Working in the Emergency Room was every bit like you would see on television with trauma cases from automobile accidents to people using the Emergency Room for non-urgent things like a sore throat or sprained ankles. I could fill this page with numerous stories of patients coming through the emergency department, however, suffice to say that all these jobs within the University Hospital seemed to be progressive and connected in some mysterious way. I went from food service to orderly, to medical records to the Emergency Room, for a total of five years. Interestingly, when I was hired for the first job at the University in food service, I went to the benefits office, and they asked me if I wanted retirement benefits with a plan called TIAA-CREF which was basically for teachers. Since the medical center was a teaching hospital, employees could sign up also. The benefits clerk assured me I would get the money back when I left employment so I thought, what the heck, I will pay into the retirement plan. When I got ready to leave the University employment some five or six years later, the clerk asked if I wanted to leave the money in the account because after five years, it is "vested" into a retirement plan, would collect interest, and I could draw on it at age 60. So, another long story made short, I left the money in my account, and the balance increased over the years while collecting interest. Since turning age 60, I have been drawing a monthly pension of a few hundred dollars a month for several years now; it seems like someone was looking out for me once again.

There are a couple more stories to go along with this prequel. For a good portion of my life, I have been single, though I knew I wanted to get married someday. For some reason, I have never had a problem having girlfriends and I don't mean to be egotistical. While working as an orderly on Station 31, neurosurgery, of the Medical Center I met a nurse named Rita, and we dated for some six months in 1972. She was a very religious person who spoke of God and unconditional love. Personally, I was on a search for the existence of God, however more in an intellectual or academic way; I wanted proof. We would have long discussions into the night about God, families, and life in general. Eventually, she persuaded me to attend an Antioch weekend at the Good Counsel Friary in Morgantown which was a weekend religious retreat, and she assured me all my questions about the existence of God would be answered. The Good Counsel Friary was staffed by Catholic priests from the Franciscan order, and I have a feeling they were accustomed to characters like me, asking all these questions and looking for proof for the existence of God! Between Rita showing me unconditional love and the Antioch weekend, I came to the realization that God does indeed exist, and I made a commitment to serve Him for the rest of my days on earth. I returned to the Catholic Church (I was a nogoer) and my life has been full of happiness and purpose since that Antioch weekend in November of 1972. Eventually, Rita and I went our separate ways, however I am convinced that she was put in my life at that time and place (Station 31 at West Virginia University Medical Center) to convert me from basically nothing to a born-again Christian. I am on the quiet side, so I don't stand on street corners and preach the gospel or wave my hands during church services, however I give it my all to serve Him through my thoughts, words, and actions. This conversion has guided me throughout my career and into public health. I could elaborate more, however that would be another book!

And yet another story. It was at the West Virginia University Medical Center where I met my wife, Karen. She was working in the outpatient clinic as a clerk, and I was working in the Emergency Department. I would be looking for medical records for patients who were in the

Emergency Department and who were recently to the outpatient clinic. She was a Christian and I was a Christian and I thought that would be a good start for a relationship. We dated for two years and became engaged for another year and married in Morgantown at St John's Catholic Church in May of 1988. We have two adult children, Becky, age 34 and Tim, age 29. I often wondered why God kept me in Morgantown for so many years and what I had to show for it. Thinking back now, I earned two degrees from the West Virginia University, a BS in Political Science and master's degree in Public Health; I had a religious conversion and now call Morgantown my Spiritual home; I met my wife, Karen, at the University Hospital; it took me so long to complete my college degrees that I earned a pension by working at the Medical Center five or more years which I receive today. Finally, I spent eight years in the US Army Reserves in Fairmont, West Virginia which coupled with my three years of active duty put me at eleven years towards the 20-year requirement to qualify for a pension and insurance benefits. So that is two college degrees, a religious conversion, a wife, and two pension plans for my time in West Virginia not to mention my first professional job at the West Virginia Department of Health (next chapter.) Not so bad after-all!

Stories from the Field – West Virginia University

West Virginia University – orderly weighing patients in the middle of the night using kilos – 1972

It was in the early 1970's when I was working as an orderly on the night shift at West Virginia University Hospital. I was working with another orderly named Tom Shih who was from Taiwan. I think he was majoring in Civil Engineering. On the night shift, we were responsible for weighing the patients who were scheduled for surgery in the morning. We went from floor to floor of the hospital and the nurses had a list of patients for us. This was in the middle of the night. The scale we used back then looked like an ironing board on wheels with a hydraulic pump, like jacking up a car to repair a flat tire. The challenge was getting the patient from the bed to the scale (ironing board); the board had to be level with the bed, and we basically rolled up the bed sheets on both sides of the patient and would slide them onto the scale. It was a rather uncomfortable and intrusive maneuver, especially at 3am in the morning. Many of the patients were overweight which made it especially challenging! For some reason, the scale registered in Kilos not pounds! I remember this one patient who asked me how much he weighed. I said I didn't know and so I asked Tom, and he would say something like 72 kilos to the patient (not pounds) in his Chinese accent. Usually, the patients would just say "Oh" and roll over and go back to sleep. This went on with all the patients who wanted to know their weight before surgery, and we just continued telling them about their weight in kilos! I am sure weighing patients today is more advanced and they use pounds instead of kilos!

West Virginia University – Suicide on Station 81

It was on the night shift when this suicide occurred. There were only two orderlies on duty in the entire hospital. I was called to station 81 which was known as the "Psych" floor. A patient named Mary, in her late or early 60's was becoming increasingly agitated and uncooperative. When I arrived on the floor, the patient was going around the nurse's station, to the dayroom, to the elevators and back again. I tried to talk with her, to slow her down, and to see what the was the matter. She went from the elevators back to the nursing station. I tried again to get her attention but this time she ran full speed from the nursing station and the entire length of the hallway and jumped headfirst through the window with a loud explosion of glass! I remember her as being a large woman (not obese) and solidly built, so the running start and momentum must have carried her through the window which was very thick glass as this was a hospital window. There was a chorus of screams and panic. She fell some eight stories below with glass all over the floor where she jumped. All that was left was a pair of slippers which remained on the floor as she went through the window. The charge nurse told me to make sure the rest of the patients in the hallway remained in their rooms and to close their doors, which I thought was a very good decision.

West Virginia University – Woodburn Hall - today

Chapter Three —

Graduate School – 1980 – 1984

By the year 1980, I had a bachelor's degree in political science from West Virginia University in Morgantown, West Virginia. However, as with any degree in Arts and Sciences one must go on to Graduate School or a technical school to get a job. I was working in the medical records department at West Virginia University Hospital at the time (1979) and thought Hospital Administration would be a good career field. Keep in mind that WVU (West Virginia University), in addition to having good football and basketball teams, is a major university with a medical school and ancillary fields of study, an approved ABA law school, engineering, business school and so forth. When I explored studies for Hospital Administration, I learned there was no curriculum for that degree! And that was that. I am not really a businessperson anyway! One of my co-workers in the medical records department suggested that I take courses in Health Education as the University was in the process of setting up a brand-new master's degree curriculum. They were looking for students to enroll in the new program with the MS degree being awarded after two semesters of graduate study and one semester of a practicum or thesis option. I was exposed to the health field in Vietnam, I enjoyed the hospital work at WVU; I liked education, so I thought here is the perfect match combining the health field with education!

The Health Education department was so new that the University didn't know where to "house" the staff of two professors, one graduate assistant and one administrative aide. Initially, the Department was housed in the agriculture department on the Evansdale campus. Students enrolling in the new Health Education curriculum had to walk through the hallways of the agriculture school with pictures of farms, tractors, and cows! Sometimes, I wondered if I was in the right place with my career goal! Much to my relief, the housing of the Health Education

Department in the School of Agriculture was temporary. West Virginia University administration officials decided to put the Health Education department with the School of Social Work, after all, Health Education is a little like social work thought school administrators. The two professors and administrative aide packed up and moved over to another building (Allen Hall) with the Social Work Department. After a year or so, it was decided that health education was not social work, so the department had to move again, this time to the School of Physical Education. As my professor said on my first day of graduate school, the hardest part of my future occupation would be defining what health educators do. We were not physical education teachers. Fast forward to today, and the Community Health Education curriculum, now a full-fledged Public Health Education program with master's and Doctorate Degrees, is housed in the Community Medicine Department which is part of the medical school. This is where the Public Health Education department belongs. Graduate studies include epidemiology, community health analysis, statistics, and Health Education Project Development. Upon completion of graduate coursework, there was the option of doing a placement in the community or doing a research project, which was a master's level thesis.

Interestingly, in undergraduate school I was an "average" student getting most "C" and occasional "B' grades with a final GPA of around 2.3 upon graduation. When I finished graduate school at WVU with my master's degree, my GPA was right around 3.5 which amazed everyone, especially my parents!

Looking back at that graduate level master's program, it was quite an experience since the initial classes were "experimental" in that we had to succeed to continue the curriculum. I recall many of the students in my classes were nurses who didn't want to do "bedside" nursing, medical students who wanted to learn about the behavior aspects of medicine, and people like me who were looking for a new and exciting career. When I finally finished my coursework and master's level thesis, I will never forget what the administrative aide, Linda Lilly, said to me: "Dave, you are a professional now," and I always remembered those words and acted accordingly throughout my professional career.

A final note on my academic preparation was that I chose to write a thesis as opposed to doing a practicum or placement in Student Health Services, the local American Lung Associate, or another voluntary health organization. It seemed like a placement in Student Health Services was basically educating students about birth control methods and Sexually Transmitted diseases. I wanted more than that so I decided on a written thesis which would take longer; however, I wanted the experience of research, investigative studies and evaluating health and medical journal articles. My thesis topic was "Psychosocial Aspects of Cardiac Rehabilitation", and it took a year and a half to complete. My research took place in the Cardiology Clinic of West Virginia University Medical Center in 1985-86. Upon completion of my research, I had to "defend" my thesis findings before a committee and I was awarded my master's degree in Community Health Education, which is today a master's degree in public health education. My thesis is hard bound, and I kept it with me throughout my career. Looking back, I think it gave me confidence as a health professional, especially when collaborating with doctors, nurses, and others in the medical field.

Stories from the field – Right Name on master's degree Diploma, but Wrong Field of Study!

On a facetious note, when I was finally awarded my master's degree in 1987, the diploma had my name on it along with the word: master's degree in **physical education**! Apparently, since the department was still housed in the School of Physical Education, that was imprinted on the diploma. My co-workers thought I was a Physical Education major! I sent it back to the University and they corrected it with "Community Health Education" which is today, master's degree of Public Health and located in the School of Medicine. Looking back on those graduate years of study, one might say that we were part of an experimental study group to see if the public health curriculum was going to succeed. We were pioneers in this new career field.

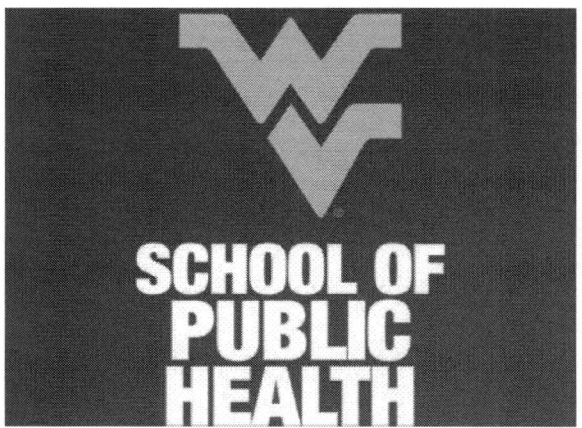

Chapter 4 -

Transition from Graduate Student to Health Professional – 1986

After I collected my data from the WVU Cardiology Clinic, I began writing my thesis and kept one eye open for a prospective job in my new occupation. Dr. Ken Simon, one of my advisors in the Health Education Department, alerted me to a job opening at the West Virginia Department of Health as an AIDS Educator. This was June of 1986. I didn't know anything about AIDS or even what the acronym meant. All I knew was that the NBC news commentator, Tom Brokaw, was reporting about some disease of unknown origin which was affecting gay men in San Francisco and Los Angeles, California. There was no cure, and the life expectancy was about two years after being diagnosed. Even though I was finishing up my thesis, I applied for the job and much to my amazement, I received an interview and was offered the position as an AIDS Educator in July of 1986! This was a Cooperative Agreement grant position awarded to the State of West Virginia by the Centers for Disease Control in Atlanta, Georgia with a starting salary of $22,000 a year. One minor detail however was that I had not finished writing my thesis, even though I had collected all the data. A long story made short; the Health Education Department allowed me to take the clinic data with me as I started my new position. I finished my thesis while on the job and later defended it with a separate trip to Morgantown later that year.

As I began my first professional job in July 1986, I read as many books about AIDS as I could find. Initially, the infection was known as GRID for Gay Related Infectious Disease and later renamed AIDS. AIDS is an acronym for Acquired Immune Deficiency Syndrome. The Centers for Disease Control in Atlanta, Georgia was the primary source of information with their

Weekly Morbidity and Mortality Report (WMMR) which was written in a language more familiar to physicians and epidemiologist. And as it turned out, my first supervisor at the West Virginia Department of Health was an MD/Epidemiologist, Dr Richard Hopkins. When we first met, I told him I really didn't like working with numbers, as I was more interested in behavior and education. He was a little taken back by that, however we managed to get over that hurdle rather quickly. He gave me a quick lecture on AIDS, especially the difference between being diagnosed with AIDS having symptoms as opposed to being infected with the AIDS virus <u>without</u> symptoms, however, still being contagious. There was a big difference there. At the time, there were very few physicians who would treat patients with AIDS for fear of getting the disease themselves and lack of medical treatment. It was incumbent upon the infectious disease physicians to establish treatment protocols. Again, in the mid and late 1980's, there was no treatment and no cure. The best physicians could do was to treat their symptoms. Clinical trials were underway at major research hospitals and the NIH (National Institute of Health).

A Quick Primer on AIDS

> There are three requirements to have an AIDS diagnosis: (1) have a positive blood lab result including Western Blot and ELISA (enzyme linked immunosorbent assay) blood test. Two positive ELISA tests were required, and the Western Blot test which was more specific and the confirmatory lab result (2) being symptomatic meaning showing physical signs of the illness like fever, chills, weight loss etc. and 3) having the diagnosis come from a medical doctor. Another indicator test is the white blood cell or CD4 test. If there is an HIV infection, the white blood cell count drops below 500 as the white blood cells fight off the HIV infection. These lab results were always guarded under lock and key at all levels of reporting. If a person had a positive blood test with no symptoms at all, they were considered HIV positive. In other words, they were not sick, however they could still transmit AIDS sexually or through IV drugs or any other bloodborne transmission.

Chapter Five -

Developing the AIDS Health Education Program for the State of West Virginia

In 1986, West Virginia was not a high incidence State with only about 25 AIDS cases. The states with the highest numbers of AIDS were New York, California, and Florida. The state of Massachusetts, especially Boston, began picking up cases also. Initially, gay men were the "high risk" population (another public health term I had to quickly learn) however other people were soon getting AIDS: intravenous drug users, people receiving blood transfusions, people with hemophilia who were getting a medication called "factor eight" which enhanced blood clotting and heterosexuals who accounted for only about three percent of all AIDS cases. Finally, there were the Haitians. For some reason, there were many cases of AIDS among the Haitians and so they were labeled a "high risk group" and not allowed in the country! However, AIDS was proliferating in the gay population by sexual (anal) intercourse and that became the priority for AIDS Prevention and Education. Prevention was the name of the game. Scientists quickly learned that AIDS was a "bloodborne" disease and in a few cases, from bodily fluids. However, the virus was mainly located in the blood. Soon IV or intravenous drug users became a high-risk group as they used needles for drug use and often shared needles which would be contaminated with the AIDS virus. So, this newly minted, master's prepared, professional health educator (myself) was faced with a monumental task, that is, prevent the spread of AIDS in the rural state of West Virginia as the very first AIDS Educator for the West Virginia Department of Health.

The first task was to locate the highest risk groups for AIDS (later named HIV for Human Immune deficiency Virus) which were gay men. In a rural state like West Virginia, with a large rural church influence, gay men were hard to find. The goal was to educate gay men about high-risk behaviors and how to protect themselves from HIV infection. For gay men, it was anal intercourse as the risk behavior, and use of a condom for the prevention. It was as simple as that; however, changing behavior is never easy. Being heterosexual, I had no idea how to approach the gay population and present prevention and education concepts. Fortunately, there was a church in Morgantown, West Virginia called the Metropolitan Community Church which was composed of mostly gay men. I set up a meeting with the pastor and we agreed that HIV/AIDS was a problem and gay men were "in denial" that it would affect them. We set up a series of "safe sex" seminars and we were successful in reaching members of the church with education and prevention seminars. All of this was rather challenging because I was "straight", and members of the Metropolitan Community Church were predominantly gay. In addition, I represented the "government" although it was the state government, so there were issues of "trust' which had to be overcome. Looking back, it was a miracle that I could conduct needs assessments and present "safe sex" seminars. The key to this successful endeavor was a good relationship with the pastor of the church who was concerned about his members engaging in risky behaviors for HIV/AIDS infection.

The second highest risk "group" was intravenous drug users who shared needles when injecting drugs. HIV/AIDS is a bloodborne disease so tiny droplets of blood could be on the shared needle. If the first drug user had AIDS, it would be transmitted to the other person, hence HIV infection. The IV drug user population was even harder to reach than the gay population. The best we could do was present AIDS Prevention and Education to drug users who were in drug rehabilitation facilities. This was met with some success, though it was limited. In larger East and West coastal cities of the United States, free needles were given on the streets to help reduce the incidence of AIDS. At the State Health Department Office, located in Charleston,

West Virginia, we had administrative support staff, however no other health professionals working directly with AIDS Education for the high-risk groups of gay men and intravenous drug users.

After the gay population and IV drug user population, there was another older population, senior citizens if you will, who were becoming infected through blood transfusions. Older people, in general, need more medical attention including surgeries requiring blood transfusions. People with AIDS were unintentionally donating blood to the nation's blood supply which was becoming contaminated with the HIV virus. Some blood donors may have been HIV positive and didn't know it. This was the year 1987. Immediately, the American Red Cross began screening all donated blood for the HIV virus. So, this was the third priority for AIDS Prevention and Education: senior citizen groups and anyone requiring a blood transfusion for any reason whether automobile accidents or routine surgery. Closely associated with the blood supply was the "factor eight" medication used by people with hemophilia. Factor eight helps with the blood clotting portion of the blood. Technically, people with hemophilia were a high-risk group also.

Finally, there was the heterosexual population which accounted for only three percent of all cases being reported to the Centers for Disease Control. Heterosexuals were not a high-risk group, and they received the least amount of attention from a health education perspective. However, there was a constant fear that AIDS would spread to the heterosexual population on a larger scale so they could not be ignored. The priorities for AIDS Education were: (1) gay men (2) Intravenous drug users (3) those in need of blood transfusion and factor eight for people with hemophilia and (4) heterosexuals. Haitians were eventually removed for the high-risk category.

Chapter Six -

Using Health Education Skills Learned in Graduate School

As a Public Health Educator, one quickly learns that three of the most important resources are: (1) time (2) allocation of resources and (3) key contacts in the community. By time, it is meant prioritizing time to reach the target population who needed prevention and education; by resources it is meant salary, office space, transportation, communications, and educational materials etc. The third resource is the key community leader to reach the high-risk populations. This might be called collaboration as well. A good example would be working with the pastor of the Metropolitan Community Church in Morgantown, West Virginia who was the key person enabling me to present the AIDS educational seminars with the church members. Please bear in mind that the AIDS epidemic was in full swing during the mid-1980's with no vaccine, no cure and the only thing working to prevent the spread of AIDS was education, especially among the high-risk groups. It should be noted that the Centers for Disease Control eventually phased out the term high risk "groups" in favor of high-risk behaviors, however for general purposes such as writing this journal, I will use "groups" for the sake of clarity.

Another additional duty of a professional health educator was to review educational materials. In the mid 1980's, VCR's and videocassette tapes were replacing the old 35mm Kodak Slide Projector and overhead projectors. The CDC provided free 35mm slides to AIDS educators, however they were loaded with charts, graphs, and numbers. Apparently, the slides were produced by epidemiologist! The videocassettes were bulky and expensive though they were attractive to the audience. However, all video cassettes had to be previewed for the target audience such as health professionals, schoolteachers, or the public. Therefore, my office was quickly filled with bookcases of video cassettes which had to be previewed before being released to public organizations. I recall some of the better videos coming from the National Institute of Health (NIH), which featured Dr. Anthony Fauci who later became an advisor to President Donald Trump when the Covid19 pandemic began in March 2019.

Being the AIDS "expert," I was called upon by the West Virginia State Department of Education to help with the development of an AIDS Curriculums for teachers throughout the state. Of importance was how AIDS was transmitted and how it was not transmitted. The curriculum had to be age and grade appropriate as to what could be said. It was like developing sex education curriculums. The terminology had to be correct and factual however not violate moral/community standards for the school. It was tricky business at best! Local school boards consisted of parents, teachers, church pastors and administrators so the wording had to be just right.

Chapter Seven -

AIDS Education for the Public

After the high risk "groups" were identified and educated about the risks of HIV infection, our attention turned to the public. Along with the tremendous loss of life and the HIV virus spreading unabated in the high-risk populations, was the epidemic of fear among the public in West Virginia and across the nation. This was a daunting task to say the least. High on the list was swimming pools; people thought the AIDS virus was in the water and if someone who was known to have AIDS went swimming in a pool, everyone jumped out! This was true for lakes as well. There were no known cases of AIDS being reported to the CDC regarding infection from a swimming pool or lake.

Next were the schools. Parents were terrified that a child with AIDS would come to school and give "it" to their children. There were no known cases of a child being infected with HIV from another child in the USA's school system. Regarding healthcare facilities and healthcare workers, I thought since they were healthcare professionals, they could figure things out. However, most could not and looked to the State Health Department for guidance and support. I prepared HIV/AIDS presentations for these organizations to allay their fears. For Emergency Responders or EMS, their concern was encountering blood or bodily fluids from someone with AIDS after an automobile accident or another traumatic event such as a gunshot wound or another injury where bleeding has occurred. Sometimes these AIDS presentations were called in-services, and I was very much in demand in 1987 as the fear of AIDS spread, even in a rural state like West Virginia. Another request for AIDS Education came from a social work agency in Charleston, West Virginia. Social Workers were concerned someone with AIDS would come into their office and touch their desk, doorknobs, or even coughing or sneezing which might spread the disease.

Another AIDS presentation was at Glenville State College located in central West Virginia. This was a student population, many of whom were sexually active. Therefore, I had to tailor my presentation to that population with an emphasis on condom use. The students were not particularly interested in abstention to prevent transmission of the HIV virus. And yet another AIDS presentation was for Albert Gallatin (Pennsylvania) Home Health Services. Home health aides were concerned about getting AIDS when changing bed sheets and touching patient personal belongings, feeding the patient, lifting the patient and so forth. So, during a course of a couple of weeks, I presented AIDS Education to Social Workers, a country interdenominational church, senior citizens, students at a medium size college, EMS or emergency medical service worker, a home health organization, and an in-service for schoolteachers. Looking back on those days, being an AIDS Educator was not a boring job given the multi-culture of the community organizations.

Stories From the Field – Presenting AIDS Education to Rural W. Va. Churches - 1987

And then there were the churches, some of whom thought HIV/AIDS was God's punishment on the gay population. When I presented AIDS education to some of the countryside churches, I always brought my wife, Karen, (my fiancée at the time) because they thought I was gay! I always made it a point to introduce my future wife to the church to assure them I was heterosexual. Thinking about it now, it was rather tenuous (whether the presentations were going to go over very well), however at the time it was serious business standing in front of the congregation talking about how AIDS is transmitted sexually.

Chapter Eight -

HIV/AIDS Ancillary Programs and Strange Bedfellows

Although I have been focusing on high-risk groups and the public, there was another area of AIDS prevention I was "privy" to. This was "contact tracing" which was conducted by Venereal Disease Investigators, later in public health known as CDI or Communicable Disease Investigators. Since AIDS was becoming primarily a sexually transmitted disease it fell in line with syphilis and venereal disease (gonorrhea). Being in the US Army for three years, I was familiar with the latter two diseases. It was part of our basic training! All three of these diseases must be reported to the State Health Department as required by law. This mandatory reporting includes hospitals, physician's office, private laboratories, health departments, and any healthcare facility performing diagnostic blood testing. A positive test for AIDS or syphilis resulted in a report to the West Virginia State Laboratory and eventually to the epidemiology department as well. The patient's name and address were entered into a confidential database. The next step in the contact tracing process is to interview the person with a positive test result to learn who his/her sexual partners were so they could be tested and ultimately stop the spread of AIDS or syphilis. The Communicable Disease Investigator makes a "home visit" to inform sexual partners of their risk (exposure) for infection. This is not a job I would want; however, I have come to admire and respect CDI's and the important work they performed to prevent the spread of AIDS in the 1980s and to the present day. It requires skill, knowledge, and bravery to knock on someone's door and tell them that they have been exposed to the AIDS virus and the CDI is requesting the names of their sexual partners. As a health educator, I never had this duty, however I have been in attendance during these contact tracing interactions both in West Virginia and South Carolina. The CDI's played an important role in preventing the spread of the AIDS virus, though they did not always receive the credit they deserved. They worked behind the scenes so to speak.

The State Laboratories in West Virginia and South Carolina.

Another strange bedfellow would be the state laboratories which performs the AIDS blood test and sends the results to the state epidemiologist and local health departments. With the AIDS epidemic spreading, these blood tests had to be guarded for confidentiality. In addition, there were logistics of shipping, receiving, and reporting blood tests which had to be accurate and verified. Blood specimens drawn on the local level had to be packaged just right and delivered to the State Lab in a timely manner to avoid clotting in shipment. Test results were mailed back to the local health facility and were critical when informing someone of their HIV blood status, whether a positive or negative result. Occasionally, there was a false positive result which required another blood test. A positive test result was given to patients by a trained HIV counselor, registered nurse or perhaps a physician. Health Educators were not called upon to give positive test results to patients, however health educators were called upon for follow up counseling, education, and prevention. Therefore, it was important for the health educator to know the blood testing process through the state laboratory both in West Virginia and South Carolina and what the test results meant. Please see the picture below.

While this picture predates my time at the West Virginia Department of Health by many years, it does show the remote location of the lab in South Charleston where blood specimens were examined for the HIV virus in 1986. The HIV positive blood test results were sent to the State Epidemiologist (my boss) and sent also to local health departments where the blood specimens originated.

The Politics of AIDS

Regarding the politics of AIDS in the mid and late 1980's, federal funding for AIDS was very slow, initially. The main beneficiary of AIDS funding were gay people or homosexuals. This led to AIDS activism, especially in the Western and Eastern coastal cities. The AIDS lobby in Washington, DC was strong and eventually, funding increased for AIDS research and for community-based organizations which promised AIDS Education for the "hard to reach" populations --gay and IV drug users. Hollywood stars, like Elizabeth Taylor, began advocating for AIDS research and she contributed large amounts of money to the "cause." Books were being written such as "And the Band Played On" by Randy Shilts which became a New York Times bestseller. An AIDS organization called "Act Up' was very vocal and instrumental in securing Federal dollars for AIDS research, medical care, and Prevention/Education programs from Congress.

I describe all of this because as a Public Health Educator, one must become familiar with all aspects of a public health problem, including politics, so prevention and education programs can be developed. Since there was no vaccine and no cure, AIDS prevention and education was the only program that was working at the time and added value to the Health Education profession.

Chapter 9 -

Off to South Carolina – 1988 – A Totally New Experience

After two years serving as West Virginia's first AIDS Educator, I decided it was time to move on. While working on the State level, there were many administrative obligations such as writing grants and progress reports which were required by the Center for Disease Control, ordering educational materials, meetings and so forth. I really wanted to get into "grass roots" health education, that is, working in a direct service role whether it was for AIDS, cardiovascular disease prevention, or another public health problem. In West Virginia, I worked with the community-based organizations who served people with AIDS. However, I met very few people who were HIV positive or who had AIDS. In a way, I wanted to get out of the office and work on the front lines of the AIDS epidemic.

A friend of mine, Jennifer Long, who was also a recent graduate of the master's level Community Health Education Program at West Virginia University, had secured a job as a District Director of Health Education in Myrtle Beach, South Carolina. The health district was part of the South Carolina's Department of Health and Environmental Control and there were three other health educator positions open in: Orangeburg, Florence and Charleston, South Carolina at the time. I was impressed with the organizational structure of the State Health Department with District level administration and then the County Health Departments. In West Virginia, there was the State Office in Charleston and then the county health departments. There were very few, if any, health educators working on the local level in West Virginia.

In South Carolina, there were Health Educators working in the Central Office located in Columbia and Health Educators working in the 13 Districts located throughout the State. In addition, Health Educators were part of the merit system with different pay grades and titles ranging from the basic health educator or bachelor's degree (Health Educator 1) level to Consultants in the Central Office who were master's prepared. I was very impressed! I applied for a position with the Edisto Health District located in Orangeburg, South Carolina as a District Director of Health Education and got the job! I supervised the staff of two other health educators, a Registered Nurse, and administrative aide. In addition, my job responsibilities included more than AIDS Education, it included heart disease prevention as well. My wife, Karen, and I were just married in May of 1988 when I was offered the position in August. Life was good. Little did I know of the challenges which lay ahead as this "city boy" from New Jersey was transitioning to a new culture in the South, home of Andrew Jackson who led South Carolina as the first State to secede from the Union in 1861 and the start of the Civil War (or as Southerners corrected me, the War of Northern aggression).

When becoming a professional Public Health Educator, an area of specialization is chosen, like physicians and nurse practitioners specializing in medicine, orthopedics, neurology, OB-GYN etc. My area of expertise became HIV/AIDS, which followed me throughout my career. However, I wanted a second area of expertise, and I chose heart disease or cardiovascular disease prevention and education. Well, South Carolina was in the "stroke belt," that is for heart disease and stroke due to a variety of reasons, mainly eating habits and sedentary lifestyles. Even though South Carolina is mostly a rural state, HIV/AIDS was and still is a BIG problem. As a matter of fact, Columbia, South Carolina has consistently ranked in the top ten cities in the United States with the number of AIDS cases per population. Columbia ranks right up there with San Francisco, Los Angles, New York City, Boston, Miami, Florida, and other East/West coast cities. So here I am, a professional health educator with two years of experience under my belt, ready to take on AIDS and rampant heart disease in South Carolina. At least I had a staff and that was a big help.

One of the first things a professional health educator does upon starting a new job is to become familiar with the community: population, industries, demographics, school systems, political organizations, churches, and city councils. In a way, we look for common interests, or allies if you will and usually people are interested in health and wellness.

We also look at the health of the community, what diseases are prevalent and what diseases can be prevented or at least managed to some degree. We also look at community resources, especially those that are health related such as hospitals, physician's offices, voluntary health organizations such as the American Red Cross and the American Lung Association, colleges and universities and local businesses.

As the new guy in town, I had the reputation as being the "AIDS expert" even to the extent that I was featured in an article in the local newspaper, the "Times and Democrat." I had to get to work right away. In the next town over (from Orangeburg) was a town called Bamberg located in Bamberg County adjacent to Orangeburg County. They were having a school board meeting to update their policy regarding a child coming to school who might have HIV/AIDS. Should the child be separated from the rest of the class? Can AIDS be transmitted by coughing and sneezing? What about the restrooms, sinks and toilet seats? At these meetings, I assured school officials that no cases had been reported to the State Health Department of children being infected by any of these transmission routes. It was primarily sexually transmitted, a bloodborne disease and through intravenous drug use. For the most part, I was trusted to provide accurate information since I worked at the state level in West Virginia and represented the South Carolina Department of Health. It was advantageous to have the school nurse present at these meetings who could verify my advice and offer support. The school nurses were usually Registered Nurses, employed by the state health department and were trusted with the health of the school children. Nurses seem to be a natural ally of public health educators.

I was soon getting calls from local colleges and universities to present AIDS Education to new students attending orientation. South Carolina State University was a frequent caller as well as the local technical schools. As these requests increased, I learned to delegate some of this work to the other Health Educators on staff. Delegation of duties and supervision was something not taught in graduate school, and I had to learn supervision on my own, including taking some night courses at the University of South Carolina.

It was a challenge working with the African American population in Orangeburg County which composed 57 percent of the population. Right away, I learned of the Orangeburg massacre of 1968 where three students from South Carolina State University were killed by police during a civil rights protest/rally near the All-Star bowling alley across the street from the campus. Although 1968 was twenty years before I arrived in Orangeburg, it was still fresh in everyone's mind. Race relations were still tense upon my arrival and that was a unique challenge within itself when presenting community health education. I quickly learned that health education had to be culturally sensitive. In addition, health education is best when it comes from a member of the culture of the target population, whether African American, Asian, White, American Indian, or any other culture. Fortunately for me, two members of the Health Education staff were African American, and they could present sensitive information, especially sexually transmitted diseases better than I.

Our Health Education Staff at the Edisto Health District began working together quite well as we developed our plans, goals and objectives for the district which was composed of three counties: Orangeburg, Calhoun, and Bamberg Counties. The counties were rural with few healthcare facilities and physicians. In Bamberg County, there was only one physician, Dr Michael Watson and two nurses who were "mid-wives" and delivered babies at home. (This was 1988). There was a county hospital in Bamberg which was originally a nursing home, all on one ground level. Most of the nurses were trained for two years at the Orangeburg-Calhoun Technical School in Orangeburg with an occasional nurse having a bachelor's degree in nursing from the University of South Carolina.

Organizational Structure of the South Carolina State Department of Health in 1988

Fortunately, our health education staff had support from the State Health Department's Central Office who were Health Education Consultants. The Health Education Consultants at the Central Office specialized in consulting for AIDS, chronic diseases (mainly heart disease and stroke), Maternal and Child health, birth control and "other" public health programs such as lead poisoning, child immunizations, child safety seats in automobiles, and oral health (brushing your teeth!). I learned that all health educators have a "funding source" according to their program i.e., the AIDS "program" or the chronic disease "program" etc. Occasionally, a health educator is funded through administrative or local funds. This is all tricky business for the District Administrator who must balance the funding sources from the Federal and State governments to ensure all employees, including health educators, are paid! Fortunately for me, my funding source was the AIDS program, and it was well funded by the federal government. This is really a caveat for Health Educators as their program funding may run out and then he/she would be out of a job!

I always admired the organizational structure of the South Carolina State Health Department back then in 1988. In addition to the District Director of Health Education was the Director of Nutrition, Director of Social Work, Director of Nursing, a District Administrator, and the District Health Director who was usually a physician. Finally, there was an Environmental Health Director whose main job appeared to be issuing septic tank permits, inspecting local restaurants for cleanliness, controlling mosquitoes, and obtaining soil samples (not sure why). There were weekly "team" meetings with sharing of ideas and decision making. Most of the health programs overlapped and required collaborative approaches to resolving community health problems. I found these meetings to be very productive and appreciated the interdisciplinary approach to resolving public health issues in the district.

AIDS in the Edisto Health District

In the Spring of 1991, HIV/AIDS was running rampant in the United States and South Carolina with no cure and no vaccine in sight. As stated previously, Columbia, SC consistently ranked in the top ten cities in the United States for the number of AIDS cases per population. Orangeburg was only 45 miles from Columbia and there was plenty of traffic between the two cities via Interstate 26. In addition, some twenty miles to the South of Orangeburg was Interstate 95 which connected New York with Miami, Florida. This was ideal for drug traffic between the two cities as Orangeburg was the halfway point and a good place to sell drugs. AIDS was so prevalent that the State Health Department hired AIDS Educators for each Health District, some 15 AIDS Educators in all! I was quite impressed with the State's response to the AIDS epidemic, especially coming from a state, West Virginia, where I was the <u>only</u> AIDS Educator. Also, in the Spring of 1991, the Ryan White AIDS Clinic was established and will be discussed further in the next chapter.

Chapter 10 -

The Ryan White AIDS Clinic – Spring 1991

Ryan White was a sixteen-year-old boy from Indiana who had hemophilia and was infected with HIV through Factor 8, the medication needed to insure blood clotting. He became a spokesperson for AIDS education and appeared on the Oprah Winfrey show in 1987. He was quite mature and articulated the myths of AIDS by making public appearances. Since there was no vaccine and no cure for AIDS, he passed away some two years after being infected. He allayed fears people had about casual transmission of the virus such as shaking hands, water fountains, using public rest rooms, coughing, and sneezing etc. The political establishment in Washington, DC was so impressed with this young man's courage that funding was appropriated for the establishment of Ryan White Clinics throughout the United States. Initially, funding went to large research centers, however eventually the monies "trickled down" to some local areas.

In the Spring of 1991, the Edisto Health District's Medical Director was a young African American woman, Dr. Constance Yearling, a recent graduate of the University of Colorado's medical school. She was very astute and alert to potential funding from the United States Congress and proceeded to help coordinate a grant with the Central Office for the establishment of an AIDS clinic at the Orangeburg County Health Department for people who were HIV positive and for those unfortunate people with full blown AIDS. Since South Carolina and Orangeburg had such high numbers of AIDS cases, the grant was approved at the Federal level and the AIDS Clinic was established in the Orangeburg County Health Department's building. An AIDS "team" was formed composed of doctors, nurses, health educators, social workers, lab technicians, and communicable disease investigators. This was pretty "heady" stuff for a relatively small, rural South Carolina town.

The challenges of a fully functional medical clinic to meet the needs of people with AIDS were great. First and foremost was to find physicians willing to treat AIDS patients. Fortunately, there was one infectious disease physician in Orangeburg who was willing to help: Dr John Samies who still practices medicine at the Orangeburg Regional Medical Hospital today. The other physicians from the Orangeburg area were general practitioners and they were just learning about AIDS. They received $75.00 per hour for their services. So, the AIDS Clinic, under Ryan White funding, was established and physicians began seeing patients on Thursday nights after regular health department hours. All of this was quite the "buzz" around the State as this was still early in the epidemic when fears and the stigma of having AIDS was still around. The patients had to use the back door of the health department, after hours, to protect their identity. Nonetheless, the AIDS Clinic at the Orangeburg County Health Department was the only hope for people with AIDS who were living in the Orangeburg area, as most physicians in South Carolina would not see AIDS patients for fear of getting AIDS themselves or their staff. Patients with AIDS would travel from neighboring counties to get into the Orangeburg clinic.

The AIDS team was led by a Registered Nurse, Bonnie Fogle, who had exceptional skills leading the team, organizing the clinic protocols, and recruiting doctors and nurses. This was a difficult task as not many health department staff wanted to work in the clinic (for fear of getting AIDS) and participation was voluntary. One of Ms. Fogle's primary tasks was to admit patients to the clinic. This was done after the lab results from the South Carolina State Laboratory were mailed to the clinic indicating a positive Western Blot and ELISA test. I always admired her counseling skills as she was the one who had to the tell the patient that their test result was

positive and for those who had full blown AIDS, life expectancy was about two or three years, a death sentence if you will.

The Health Educator's clinic role was diverse ranging from providing health education/risk reduction counseling to the patients during clinic to running the support group. Preventing the spread of AIDS was of paramount importance and it was incumbent upon the health educator to talk with patients about condom use, sexual abstinence, and a reduction of sexual partners. Sometimes it was individual patient education, sometimes it was group education which preceded the support group. In addition, the Health Educator talked with patients about the benefits of nutrition to boost their immune system, exercise, and taking medication (though there was only one medication approved for AIDS treatment at the time called AZT). Another subject the Health Educator had to learn was last wills, living wills and the subject of life insurance. It was impossible to get life insurance if one had a life expectancy of two years. I will never forget the anguish, the fear of death, and sufferings experienced by these young gay men who drove many miles in hopes of receiving medical treatment, a cure and living a long life. In addition, there were many heterosexual women who were infected with the AIDS virus by a sexual partner who may have been bisexual or an intravenous drug user. Some of the HIV positive women had children and the children had to be tested for the HIV virus as well. In a way, health education was evolving into patient education which was becoming another purview for the profession. Some nurses were reluctant to accept patient educators who were not nurses, however they soon relinquished the task as they were busy with their other nursing duties. Most of the patients in the AIDS Clinic were receptive to health education as they wanted to talk with someone about their HIV/AIDS condition.

The Ryan White "AIDS Clinic" continued operating, receiving federal funding right up to the year 2000 and shortly thereafter. By that year, medications were being developed to slow down the replication of the HIV virus in the human body and the sense of urgency was slowing. In a way, the new medications, called protease inhibitors, would buy time for the patients though today they are quite effective controlling the replication of the virus. Eventually, the AIDS Clinic at the Orangeburg County Health Department closed its' doors around 2005 and people with HIV were case managed by another newly formed organization called Hope Health, Inc. Interestingly, the CEO of Hope Health Inc. was a social worker for the Ryan White Clinic in Orangeburg before he became CEO of Hope Health, Inc. Hope Health, Inc. began receiving Ryan White funding in 2006 and conducted a weekly "AIDS Clinic" in Orangeburg in another location and it is still in operation today. However, Hope-Health Inc. today, is primarily case management as medical services are provided by the Family Health Centers, Inc. a Federally Qualified Health Center located in Orangeburg (see next Chapter).

Unsung Heroes of the Ryan White Clinic

Two of the unsung heroes of the Ryan White Clinic were Vivian Curven and Amy Ayers. Vivian received her bachelor's degree in nursing from the University of South Carolina and Amy received her RN degree from Orangeburg-Calhoun Technical College. Both were "tuberculosis nurses" who took care of patients who had both AIDS and tuberculosis. Tuberculosis is a highly contagious disease spread by coughing and sneezing. It affects the lungs and can be fatal if not treated with medication. Frequently, patients with tuberculosis and AIDS couldn't even make it to the Thursday night clinic because they were so sick, therefore the nurses had to make home visits to make sure the patients with "TB" took their medicine, usually Isoniazid (INH) or rifampin (RIF). In a way, Vivian and Amy were at double risk for infection: tuberculosis and

HIV/AIDS. They had to be sure to use personal protective equipment when going into the homes and interacting with the patients. Thinking back, I really admired these two nurses who were fresh out of nursing school and taking care of patients with both AIDS and tuberculosis at the peak of the AIDS epidemic.

The Ryan White Clinic, established at the Orangeburg County Health Department in 1991 was so successful that the New York Times ran a full feature article with quotes and praises from then President Bill Clinton. Looking back, it was quite a privilege to have been a part of this AIDS team. Please see a below picture of the Orangeburg County Health Department.

The back entrance of the Orangeburg County Health Department where AIDS patients entered the building after hours to protect their identity and HIV status.

Different Faces of AIDS are Conjured Up by Politicians

New York Times reprint

About the Archive

This is a digitized version of an article from The Times's print archive, before the start of online publication in 1996. To preserve these articles as they originally appeared, The Times does not alter, edit or update them.

When Senator Jesse Helms explained why he wanted to reduce Federal spending on AIDS care and research, he conjured an image of homosexuals "deliberately engaging in unnatural acts" who had nothing but their own "disgusting, revolting conduct" to blame for contracting the disease.

When President Clinton sought to rebut the Senator, he conjured a different image: that of "Debbie," a 27-year-old woman in a rural area near Orangeburg, S.C., about 75 miles northwest of Charleston, who was served by a county clinic made possible through the Ryan White Comprehensive AIDS Resource Emergency Act of 1990.

The act, named for an Indiana teen-ager who died of AIDS, provided $633 million this year in care and assistance for people with AIDS or H.I.V., the virus that causes AIDS. The law is due to expire in September and the move to reauthorize it has stalled in Congress, in part because of objections raised by Senator Helms, a North Carolina Republican.

During the debate this week over the future of AIDS financing, the disease was given the face both of sexually active gay men and of impoverished rural women.

In fact, AIDS has many faces. Of 80,691 AIDS cases reported last year by the Federal Centers for Disease Control and Prevention, 43 percent involved men who had sex with other men, 27 percent involved users of injected drugs and 5 percent involved both. Another 10 percent involved men and women who were exposed through heterosexual sex. Children whose mothers had H.I.V. accounted for 1 percent, as did people who received contaminated blood or tissue.

"Not everybody who has AIDS gets it from sex or drug needles," Mr. Clinton said on Thursday, in a speech at Georgetown University. "But secondly, and more to the point, gay people who have AIDS are still our sons, our brothers, our cousins, our citizens. They're Americans, too. They're obeying the law and working hard. They are entitled to be treated like everybody else."

With that, the President addressed the other question on which the debate over AIDS financing has turned: Are people with AIDS treated like everybody else when it comes to Federal spending, or do they receive a disproportionately large share?

Senator Helms said he wanted to amend the reauthorization bill to reduce the amount spent on AIDS in relation to heart disease and cancer. "I'm going to try to get some equity for people who have had heart trouble," he said.

The American Heart Association estimated that the Department of Health and Human Services spent $36,763 in research for every AIDS or H.I.V.-related death in 1993, in contrast to $3,708 for every death from cancer, $1,032 for every death from heart disease and $731 for every death from stroke.

But the President said on Wednesday in a letter to Senator Bob Dole, the majority leader, that when Federal spending on treatment, prevention, Medicaid, Medicare and other income supplements was added to the research figures, a different picture emerged. According to Mr. Clinton's calculations, $6 billion was spent on AIDS this year, $17.5 billion on cancer and $38 billion on heart disease.

Dr. Sidney C. Smith Jr., president of the American Heart Association and chief of cardiology at the University of North Carolina, said more Federal support for research on heart disease was badly needed. "But I don't think the answer to this is to neglect the funding of other important disease entities," Dr. Smith said. "So, I would disagree that we need to stop other important programs, such as cancer or AIDS. We, as a society, need to recognize the value and importance of research."

The vice president for government relations of the American Cancer Society, Kerrie B. Wilson, said: "In terms of medical research overall, we're not going to get anywhere by fighting the disease war."

And Patricia S. Fleming, the national AIDS policy director, sounded the same theme. "No one can win if we start pitting one disease against another," she said.

Ms. Fleming said that in 1994, the Ryan White law provided care and services to more than 200,000 people with AIDS and H.I.V. who were not covered, or only partly covered, by insurance.

These recipients included "Debbie," the pseudonym for the 27-year-old South Carolina woman whom the President mentioned.

Mary Ann Berry, the nurse who heads the team at the AIDS clinic in the Orangeburg County Health Department, said in a telephone interview yesterday that she was with Debbie at the time of her death last December.

"We're like one big family," Ms. Berry said. "It's not like a care giver-patient. Nobody's number. Everybody's a person."

The clinic operates six days a month, with a staff of seven and doctors who are brought in on rotation. It has served 202 patients with AIDS and 530 patients with H.I.V., said Leonard F. Rice, district health director for the Edisto Health District, which includes Orangeburg. The district received $150,000 through the Ryan White act.

"In so many cases the individuals would not have access to any care whatsoever if it were not for the clinic we hold here," Mr. Rice said.

Besides children born to mothers with H.I.V., Ms. Berry said, patients at the clinic ranged in age from 13 to 78. While most cases involved men, she said, "our female population is rising tremendously."

"We're dealing with very indigent people," Ms. Berry said. "Some of them you can't educate. We've got people out here you've got to pull out from the cracks. They're scared. They don't understand."

"If they pull the money away, what are our people going to do?" she asked. "Where are they going to go? I'm the one who has to look them in the face. I used to have to say, 'Sorry, if you have H.I.V., there's no place I can send you.' I hate to think I'd have to go back to doing that again."

A version of this article appears in print on July 8, 1995, Section 1, Page 7 of the National edition with the headline: Different Faces of AIDS Are Conjured Up by Politicians. Order Reprints |

25 Years Ryan White HIV/AIDS Program
Moving Forward with CARE: Building on 25 Years of Passion, Purpose, and Excellence

Community Based AIDS Prevention/ Education and the Ryan White Clinic

While the Ryan White "AIDS Clinic" was operating very smoothly, an additional link was necessary for community prevention/education, especially for those testing positive for the virus, people who were at risk for infection and those patients in need of support services such as housing, social services, disability and so forth. An AIDS "consumer group" was established and led by Pat Kelly who was HIV positive herself. She did not let an HIV/AIDS diagnosis interfere with her mission to provide education and support for people with AIDS, especially women. Pat attended numerous conferences nationwide and achieved national recognition for her efforts. She is still active today promoting AIDS prevention and education and helping people with AIDS.

Stories from the field – Transporting blood specimens to the South Carolina State Laboratory late at night after the Thursday evening clinic

Another one of my "other duties as assigned" as a public health educator was transporting blood specimens from HIV positive patients to the South Carolina State Laboratory located in Columbia, South Carolina. The blood had to be delivered that evening so that it could be examined the next morning (Friday)for white blood counts and other serological testing. Time was of the essence as if it was not delivered in a timely manner (overnight) it would "clot" by Monday morning and the lab results would not be accurate. As the story goes, the blood specimens were in vacutainer tubes, wrapped carefully, placed in a Styrofoam container packed with dry ice and placed in the trunk of my car ready to make the trip from Orangeburg to Columbia after the Thursday night clinic which could be anywhere from 7 to 9pm. Frequently, I would be driving my wife's car which was a red compact Renault Alliance. She had a few misgivings about using her car to transport HIV blood in the trunk of her car, however I assured her that it was for a worthy cause. As the story continues, after making the one-hour trip to Columbia via Interstate 26, I would arrive later in the evening at the State Lab, in the dark, and of course the lab was closed. I had to drive around back and place the Styrofoam container of blood specimens in a "drop box" on the wall like what one would see at the post office. There was a sign over the drop box which said for "animal heads" because the state lab would examine animal heads for rabies! Anyway, the place was kind of creepy and I got out of there fast! I will never forget the clinic supervisor, Sue Plunkett, RN, telling me to drive carefully as she didn't want me to have an automobile accident on Interstate 26 with HIV positive blood in the trunk of the car!

Chapter 11

Health Promotion in the Edisto Health District – 1989

As Public Health Education began to grow as a recognized profession, there was another competing field called Health Promotion which began to flourish simultaneously. Health Educators viewed this field as marketing and advertising rather than Health Education. Health Education is defined by Laurence Green, DrPH, as a "voluntary change of behavior," There was controversy whether to call our profession Health Education or Health Promotion! On a larger scale, Health Promotion was becoming more recognizable as a concept. The Health Educator was thought of as a school health teacher. Eventually, in the late 1980's the profession became known as Health Promotion and Education which is now used by major schools of Public Health. It was a compromise of sorts. Soon, block grants started coming into the South Carolina State Health Department from the federal government for heart disease prevention and education through the Health Promotion program.

South Carolina was and still is known as the "stroke belt" because of the high numbers of heart related deaths and disability, including stroke. Monies became available to all of South Carolina's Health Districts for Health Promotion activities such as worksite cholesterol testing and education and community coalition building. Most of the Health Promotion activities were guided by the State Health Department's Central Office. On the local level (our District), smoking cessation classes were offered to residents. The American Lung Association program was used, and we were quite successful with many people giving up smoking. It looked like Health Promotion was here to stay and we all became accustomed to the new terminology: Health Promotion and Education.

In a way, Health Educators had to accept the Health Promotion "program" on the State level because Health Promotion was the funding source (the block grants from the Federal government). If you wanted the money and wanted a salary, one had to go along with the health promotion program (whether you liked it or not), especially if one was hired for that specific program (Health Promotion). This is the caveat and conundrum for health educators because when the program funding runs out, the health educator may be out of a job! This is the downside of choosing Public Health Education as a career. Fortunately, health educators can easily acquire skills for other areas such as corporate wellness, school health, voluntary agencies, and other community health programs.

As Health Promotion evolved in the district, health coalitions were formed. These were community-based organizations which were more in keeping with community health education. The Edisto Health coalition was formed by another Health Educator/Nutritionist, and community members took "ownership" of their health by conducting health fairs and other community health activities. The coalition served the community as a non-profit organization and maintained an office in downtown Orangeburg for several years and is still in operation today.

Chapter 12 -

The Maternal and Child Health Program – Edisto Health District

South Carolina was known for its high infant mortality rate, that is, babies who died prematurely before birth or did not survive its first year of life. The infant mortality rate was about nine percent in the Edisto Health District in 1990, which was higher than other Health Districts in the State. The health behaviors contributing to infant mortality were mothers who smoked cigarettes while pregnant, consumed alcoholic beverages, indulged in illicit drug use, poor nutrition, obesity, and general lack of prenatal care. By prenatal care, it means seeing a physician while pregnant and receiving care for nine months until delivery. When looking at the unhealthy behaviors for pregnant women attending the maternity clinic, it was realized this was another job for health education.

The Orangeburg County Health Department had a maternity clinic once a week. There was also a weekly maternity clinic at the Bamberg County Health Department and the Holly Hill Clinic which was part of the Edisto Health District. These maternity clinics were funded by the State Health Department's Bureau of Maternal and Child Health with block grants coming from the Federal Government's Health and Human Services Department. As a Health Educator, I provided the prenatal education which included fetal growth and development, nutrition, importance of appointment keeping, breast and bottle feeding, birth control methods, and taking care of a baby during the first year of life. This program was of such importance that Health Educators could bill for their services and the Health Department would be paid from the block grants through the Central Office. This enhanced the importance of health education and helped reduce infant mortality in the district.

The Maternity Clinic was "run" by nurses who provided the prenatal care. When the patient reached the eighth or ninth month they were transferred to a local physician for their final months of care and were given Medicaid. However, for the most part, the maternity nurses provided the prenatal care, sometimes right up to the ninth month of pregnancy. This was true for the neighboring Bamberg County Health Department as well and the Holly Hill Clinic.

The Prenatal Mission – A Volunteer Organization

Another interesting facet of the maternity clinic was the Prenatal Mission. This was a volunteer church-based organization affiliated with a predominately black Methodist Church in Orangeburg. All were volunteer women who helped the patients with transportation, daycare services, clothing for the baby and general supportive care. Ultimately, they narrowed their mission to establishing a day care center within the Health Department's building. The idea was to offer daycare if the patient had young children and needed to keep her appointment. They also promoted early prenatal care and the maternity clinic at health fairs and other public events. I bring this up because Health Educators frequently work with community-based volunteer organizations to achieve goals like the reduction of infant mortality and morbidity. Since I was working in the maternity clinic, I was the liaison for the Prenatal Mission. Thus, another job for the Health Educator. I did all this while being the District Director of Health Education, working at the AIDS Clinic and supervising the Health Promotion program in the district.

Looking back on the maternal health experience at the time in 1989, I was amazed at the lack of prenatal care these young women received and the health risks to their developing babies.

Some women who lived in the rural parts of Orangeburg and Bamberg Counties, did not come into the maternity clinic until the later months of their pregnancy. In Bamberg County, the two midwives were delivering babies in the home.

I bring these issues to the forefront, not to be critical but to stress the importance of Health Education both in the community and the clinic setting. The health educator also had to address health problems simultaneously: prenatal health education and HIV/AIDS education. The Health Educator had to be knowledgeable about both health programs to do his/her job. Occasionally, a pregnant woman was HIV positive **and** a patient in the maternity clinic. This presented an immediate risk for the developing baby who might be HIV positive as well. Upon birth, the baby was sent to a special pediatric unit of Richland Memorial Hospital (now PRISMA Health) for HIV screening and monitoring. Fortunately, many babies who initially tested positive were only showing the baby's mother's "antibodies" and later reverted to a HIV negative status. Joanne Wouri, RN, was the primary health professional in Columbia who coordinated the prenatal AIDS program between the Ryan White Clinic in Orangeburg and Richland Memorial Hospital's pediatric clinic.

The Maternal and Child Health "Lead" Program

Another program was the Child Health program, and it was usually coupled as the Maternal and Child Health program. An interesting aspect of this program was the **lead** program. By lead it means the compound, lead, which is found in dried paint. This is relevant because poverty is so widespread in South Carolina that some people live in substandard housing with old paint which is chipping and peeling away. Toddlers who were hungry would eat the paint, thus ingesting the lead which caused health problems such as developmental delays, both physically and mentally. Thus, another job for the Health Educator!

As stated previously, these programs usually came with funding from the State Health Department's Central Office who get their money from the Federal Government. However, the money is not always given to the Districts and Health Departments, one must write a grant demonstrating the need and how those funds will be spent. Not all Health Districts received funds to prevent lead poisoning. It was usually the larger cities like Charleston, SC who received those kinds of funds and hence they had a "**Lead**" Health Educator!

Another job for the Health Educator was childhood immunizations, at least in the maternity clinics. This was the basic series of immunizations for childhood diseases like measles, chicken pox etc. These basic immunizations were required before beginning the school year or daycare. The childhood immunization program was part of the Child Health program which was connected to the Maternal Health program. If a Health Educator worked in the Maternal Child Health Program, that person had a full-time job, hence a Maternal and Child Health Educator.

Beyond the South Carolina Department of Health and Edisto Health District

After working for six years for the South Carolina Department of Health and the Edisto Health District, I thought it was time for a change. After all, I worked all the programs—AIDS, Cardiovascular Disease Prevention, Health Promotion, and Maternal and Child Health. I was looking for some new challenges in Public Health in addition to the SC State Health Department's programs. As stated previously, working for a State Health Department, Health

Educators are limited to the health programs which receive funding from the Federal or State governments.

In Orangeburg, there was an organization called The Family Health Center, Inc. which was a Federally Qualified Health Center and offered a variety of medical services to low-income residents of Orangeburg and surrounding counties. In September of 1996, they had a job opening for a clinical health educator, so I applied for the position, got an interview and sure enough, was offered the position. I made a lot of good friends at the Edisto Health District and after six years, I was a little reluctant to leave. However, the Family Health Center, Inc. offered new challenges and new fields of health education such as diabetes, hypertension, obesity, and all the so-called chronic diseases. I accepted the position in October of 1996 and began work after giving two weeks' notice to the Edisto Health District.

Stories From the Field - 12-Year-old girl in Maternity Clinic

The patients who attended the maternity clinic were mostly young, African American girls who had boyfriends (not husbands) as the father of the baby. Sadly, the father was frequently absent and left the scene once the baby was born, if not before. I will never forget a 12-year-old girl from Bowman, SC who was sitting in the waiting room, dangling her feet from the chair and had no idea why she was there. She didn't know she was pregnant, and someone had to tell her.

Stories from the Field – Edisto Health District – 1988

Hurricane Hugo – September 9, 1989

   As if transitioning to a new culture and new job at the Edisto Health District wasn't enough, we had Hurricane Hugo in September of 1989. Hurricane Hugo was a huge category 5 hurricane which slammed into the South Carolina coastal town of Charleston, SC with winds around 150 mph. My wife, Karen, and I were living in an apartment complex in Orangeburg, some 75 miles from Charleston when Hugo hit the coast. Winds in Orangeburg topped 80 miles per hour which came in the middle of the night. I was watching an NBC news special report around 11pm when we lost electricity, then we turned on our flashlights and lit candles. I stayed up all night to make sure everyone was safe including our daughter, Becky, who was a little over a year old. We survived the storm however trees were down everywhere and there was no electricity. Since it was a weekday, I went to my office the next morning at the Edisto Health District to inspect for damage. No windows were broken, however there was some water leaking from the roof, so I reported that to the District Administrator who lived in Holly Hill, SC. The following day, the district's "core staff" (including myself), met to develop any necessary plan of action or response to Hurricane Hugo. The Director of Environment Services came up with a good idea to educate the public about food safety since there was no electricity and food could spoil in refrigerators rather quickly resulting in food poisoning. We developed a series of PSA's or Public Service Announcements regarding food safety. The PSAs were broadcast over the local radio stations. Thus, another job for the Health Educator! After a day or two, electricity was restored, and the Edisto Health District resumed operations. There was a very unfortunate and sad incident where a District employee, a young girl, who was a lab tech lost her life the day after Hugo when she and some others were using a chain saw to remove downed trees in her neighborhood. Apparently, she was caught under a huge tree stump which collapsed on her!

   Hurricane Hugo inflicted more damage along the SC coast including Charleston, Hilton Head, and the Beaufort area. I was never afraid of Hugo, after all I went through the Vietnam war, however Hurricane Hugo got my attention and I have become a keen hurricane watcher since then!

Chapter 13 -

<u>The Family Health Centers, Inc, 1996 – 1999</u>

Our journey continues from the West Virginia Department of Health to the South Carolina Department of Health to the Family Health Centers, Inc. in Orangeburg, South Carolina. It should be noted that the organizational structure is different for the Family Health Center in that it is a non-profit organization governed by a Board of Directors. The Family Health Center is a Federally Qualified Community Health Center and receives some federal funding from the US Congress under an act called 330 federal funding. For this reason, people think the Family Health Center is a Federally run organization. It is true that some of the funding comes from Washington, DC, however the Family Health Center bills for Medicare, Medicaid, and private insurance. They also charge a fee for clinic visits on a "sliding scale' based on income. An interesting note here is that a health educator was required to be on staff to receive federal funding and I thought that was a nice boost or compliment to our profession!

The Family Health Center, Inc. was a different environment from the state health departments. For openers, there was some confusion when I did the paperwork for personnel and payroll. The confusion centered around whether I was a professional with a salaried position or hourly wage employee. That was cleared up right away by the Human Resource director since I had a master's degree which is considered a professional position. Also, I had the title of Director of Health Education Services.

As a Federally Qualified Health Center, the Family Health Center had physicians, Nurse Practitioners, nurses and clinics for General Medicine, Pediatrics, OB-GN, Dentistry, and Urgent Care. In addition to the main clinic in Orangeburg, there were satellite clinics located in neighboring towns of Vance, St. Mathews, Norway, and St. George, South Carolina. The General Medicine clinic in Orangeburg was in operation every day from 8am to 5pm and many of the patients had diabetes, hypertension, elevated cholesterol, were overweight, and/or smoked cigarettes. The satellite clinics had patients with the same health problems. There was no shortage of work for the Health Educator!

While there was some community health education, my focus was the General Medicine clinic. The clinic was staffed by physicians who were frequently from other countries like India, Africa, or Vietnam. There were nurse practitioners working at the clinic as well. Since most of my health education was community based, I had to learn patient education which was about disease etiology for diabetes, heart disease, and other chronic diseases such as arthritis and osteoporosis. For the most part, I had to self-educate myself about these diseases so that I could provide the education patients needed to prevent or manage their disease. The Family Health Centers was kind enough to send me to several conferences both locally and in other states to broaden my scope and knowledge about these diseases.

Community Health Education at the Family Health Center, Inc.

Another interesting aspect of working at the Family Health Centers was the mobile van. The mobile van was basically a traditional camper converted into a mobile clinic. In addition to being the health educator, I was the driver of the van! We went into rural communities on Saturdays and screened residents for high blood pressure and high cholesterol. If someone had an elevated reading, they were referred to their physician and if they did not have a physician, they were referred to the Family Health Center or a neighboring satellite clinic. I provided the onsite patient education for high blood pressure which usually consisted of salt reduction in their diet, daily exercise, smoking cessation, stress management and medication taking if necessary. One screening was for an American Indian community near Santee, South Carolina. Historically, there was a tribe of Santee Indians living in the area and they were in the process of documenting their ancestry, perhaps in the hopes of getting recognition as a tribe and receive Federal funding. Nonetheless, we did our hypertension screening and identified several persons with high blood pressure and referred them to the nearest health facility for treatment. We had to document everything including their name and blood pressure result. We then made referrals to their private doctor or local community health center.

School Health Education at the Family Health Center

The Family Health Centers had a very active grant writing team. They secured a federal grant for teen pregnancy prevention and guess who was called to provide that education? As the only Health Educator on staff, I was called to the local high school to talk with students about pregnancy prevention, sexually transmitted diseases, and the importance of birth control if they were sexually active. I was careful not to advocate a birth control method, only to carefully asking them whether they should be sexually active and, for the girls, the "consequences" of becoming pregnant, like dropping out of school and readiness to become a parent. I was called upon to talk with not only young teenage girls, but young men or "boys" as well. Here is another feather in my cap of an older white man talking with a predominately black teen-age student population about sex education at that! Looking back, most of the "kids" were quite receptive and even talkative about this subject. I don't think many parents or teachers sat down and talked with their children about such a sensitive subject. Eventually, other Family Health Center staff became involved in the school health education program which expanded to satellite clinics. A nurse practitioner was hired to visit some of the other satellite clinics and talked to the students about birth control methods.

Migrant Health Program at the Family Health Center

As a Federally Qualified Health Center, funds became available from the Federal government for health services for migrant workers also referred to as seasonal farmworkers, most of whom were from Mexico and some from neighboring Central America countries. The migrant workers picked cantaloupe, strawberries, green beans, peaches and whatever was in season at the time. Some stayed in the Orangeburg/Bamberg and Calhoun County area while others moved up the East Coast all the way to North Carolina, Virginia, and upstate New York. The health problems experienced by the migrant workers were numerous, however diabetes and hypertension seemed to be prevalent in this population. The Family Health Center had the mobile van, and the migrant health program was staffed by Dr. Jose Rivera, myself, a medica assistant and a Spanish translator. We traveled to the various "camps" where the migrants worked and lived and proceeded to perform blood pressure and diabetes screenings. Those with elevated readings were referred to the Family Health Center's main site or a satellite clinic. As the staff Health Educator, my job was to educate the migrant workers about the risks of high blood pressure, diabetes, and other chronic diseases. This was a challenging task as most of the migrant workers did not speak English and many could not read or write. There was one migrant worker who had extremely high blood sugar readings and when I asked him about his diet, he said he ate several cantaloupes a day! Cantaloupes contain large amounts of sugar or fructose and contribute to diabetes. He complained of tiredness and dizziness.

While the mobile van was available, there were occasions when we skipped the van, and I used my own car to travel to some of the camps in the Bamberg area with a premed student, Daniele Davis, who happened to be from the Orangeburg area. She spoke fluent Spanish and we visited some of the Bamberg area migrant camps and performed Health Education Assessments after work hours. For the most part, the migrant workers were receptive to our services.

Stories from the Field – Men from Mexico "breaking in" horses for competition!

Another interesting excursion was to a horse farm in Calhoun County. We drove the mobile van to the horse farm, and to my amazement men from Mexico were "breaking in" horses to race competitively in the Kentucky Derby, Belmont Stakes, and other major horse racing events. And they were quite skilled in their profession! At any rate, we proceeded to perform our health screenings and health education assessments. We identified several men with high blood pressure and potential diabetics. It should be noted that we had to get permission from the horse farm owner to drive onto the property and to be careful not to interfere with their work. We usually performed the health screenings during their lunch break. Those identified with high blood pressure and diabetes were referred to their physician if they had one (usually they did not) or the Family Health Center's Calhoun County satellite clinic just like the other screenings.

Primary Care at the Family Health Center

Primary care is like a family doctor who takes care of general health problems. As the clinic health educator, my focus was individual patient education in the general medicine clinic attended by some 40 patients per day, Monday through Friday. There was no shortage of patients with diabetes, high blood pressure, heart disease, lung disease due to smoking and other general ailments. As a health educator, it is important to develop and maintain professional relationships to perform our jobs and achieve desired outcomes with the patients. Physicians and nurse practitioners would see the patient in clinic and then call or refer the patient to the health educator. The referral was made in real time, that is, I was called to the medicine clinic and walked the patient back to my office for the education. If I was busy with another patient, the physician would tell the medical assistant to walk the patient to my office.

It was in this primary care setting that I learned about the suffering and illness brought on by diabetes and the other heart related illnesses which contributed to the high incidence of early death and morbidity in South Carolina. These were the faces behind the statistics so to speak. Referrals from the General Medicine Clinic came on a regular basis from Dr. Usha Kondapenini who was originally from India and had been in the United States for several years. In addition, the nurse practitioners made regular referrals as well. I would see seven to nine patients per day in my office, however sometimes I would see the patients in the clinic exam rooms. Patient education documentation consisted of the assessment, intervention and plan, and evaluation. Patient education usually involved nutrition, exercise and proper medication taking. This sounds like an oversimplification; however, these are the cornerstones of prevention and management of most of the chronic diseases including obesity. I quickly had to learn how to document my patient interactions using the traditional SOAP note which was an acronym for Subjective-Objective-Assessment-Plan. Physicians and nurses use this format when documenting their interactions with the patients also. I learned medical terminology, abbreviations and writing in a concise manner. All the medical records (at the time) were the traditional "paper" charts, so I had to be familiar with retrieving and returning medical records from the medical records department.

Seeing patients in the clinic taught me to be an active listener. Every patient had a story to tell including socio-economic hardships, illness in the family, bills to pay, strained family relationships, multiple health problems and so forth. In Health Education, we call these barriers to learning. As a health educator, I had to sort through all of this before beginning patient education. Frequently, I made referrals to the Social Worker, Misty Tate, MSW, whose office was right around the corner from mine. I remember one patient who came to my office in tears after being newly diagnosed with diabetes. When I asked her why she was crying, she said that no one has ever shown her concern for her health.

Health Educators are not miracle workers as we depend on "voluntary change in behavior." Health Educators facilitate behavior change by a variety of means: listening, assessing knowledge of the disease, motivation to change behavior, consequences of not changing behaviors (health deteriorates) and continued support and encouragement after the patient leaves the clinic. Some patients do well, and others do not; it depends on their attitude and their willingness to learn and improve their health. In general, I would say that out of a hundred patients, 1/3 do nothing or don't care about their health; 1/3 try, however don't succeed, and give up and another 1/3 of the patients listen and make changes to improve their health. For the health educator, seeing patients lose weight, quit smoking, improve blood glucose levels for diabetes and seeing improved blood pressure, makes the job rewarding and satisfying. As a physician once told me, my job as a health educator is more important than his because we are trying to prevent the disease, or at least, manage it through behavior change. And I would also say, jokingly, the doctor has the easy job; writing the prescription and saying come back in two weeks!

Beyond Primary Care

As if the General Medicine Clinic at the Family Health Center didn't keep me busy enough, I received calls from the Pediatric Clinic and the OB-GYN Clinic. I wondered why a health educator would be called to a pediatric clinic. Pediatrics is considered ages 1 to 19. There were young men and women in the pediatric clinic who were overweight and obese, many who were pre-teen adolescents. I remember one 12-year-old boy who was overweight and had high blood pressure! He had no idea what high blood pressure meant. Frequently, the parents accompanied the patients to my office. Health Education was basically following the food pyramid and limiting calories along with daily exercise. Most of the young patients were African American but not all of them.

My final health education endeavor was in the maternity clinic at the Family Health Center. Since I worked in the maternity clinic at the Edisto Health District, I was qualified to provide prenatal health education to the Family Health Center's OB patients. Again, this was basic fetal growth and development, nutrition for pregnant mothers, importance of prenatal care and even some labor and delivery concepts. I never became bored as a health educator whether in the clinic or community setting!

The Plight of the Uninsured Patients

I use the word "plight" because most of the patients did not have health insurance, though some had Medicare (mostly for seniors and those on disability) or Medicaid (state run insurance program). A few of the patients had Blue Cross Blue Shield if they were a state employee. Even prescription medications were difficult to obtain due to their high cost. Not everyone had Medicare or Medicaid as there are strict eligibility requirements for these programs. Frequently, patients needed to see a specialist physician such as cardiologist, urologist, or orthopedics, however private physicians in the community were reluctant to see patients without insurance or even Medicare and Medicaid patients. Thus, the "plight" of the patient who needed further treatment from a specialist physician. A disease like diabetes requires annual eye exams, a visit to the podiatrist for foot exams, and there are many complications of the disease which require specialization such as a kidney specialist. Without further medical care, the patient's health would deteriorate and eventually die an early death. In a way, this was my introduction to the health care system in the United States. Even medications were not affordable in the late 1990's as generic medications were just coming in along with Plan "D" for Medicare recipients.

With these limitations, doctors having difficulty making specialty referrals and the cost of medications, health education and prevention became even more important to prevent these diseases from becoming worse. When looking at the admission and discharge summaries from the local hospitals in Orangeburg, the summaries revealed many diabetes and heart disease related medical problems: stroke, leg amputation, blindness, kidney failure and so on. Where were the health and patient educators?

By December of 1999, I was getting a little tired (health professionals call it "burn out") and I was ready to move on. There was a job opening in the Health Promotion section in Blue Cross Blue Shield of Columbia, I applied for the position and to my amazement, I got the job! This was in a department of Blue Cross and Blue Shield called "HMO Blue."

The Family Health Centers, Inc. today in Orangeburg, South Carolina.

Chapter 14

Interim Jobs -Blue Cross Blue Shield – January – September 2000

I started my new position in the Health Promotion section of Blue Cross Blue Shield in January of 2000 thinking I would be implementing worksite wellness programs such as cholesterol education and screening and smoking cessation classes. The worksites were different Blue Cross Blue Shield "members" or companies, if you will, who desired to improve the health of their employees. I enjoyed direct services and thought this would be an enjoyable job with a good salary and with a prestigious corporation. To make a long story short, I was assigned to a "cubby hole" office (a cubicle), the kind you see in big corporate rooms. Basically, they were portable wall dividers and not an actual office. Conversations could easily be overheard and there was no privacy. Health promotion was to be over the telephone whether smoking cessation or weight reduction. There was no face-to-face interaction like in the clinics at the Family Health Center and Ryan White Clinic. I didn't last very long in this kind of environment. I interacted with some Registered Nurses; however, they were busy on the telephone discussing billing codes and information from the physician's offices.

I stayed busy by writing the newsletter for our department called HMO Blue and made phone calls to "members" to help with smoking cessation and some diabetes education. Blue Cross Blue shield hired a RN nurse for the diabetes education which was all telephone education. Perhaps today, we could call that telehealth! Working at Blue Cross Blue Shield was a corporate environment. The entire indoor décor was gray. One could not look out the windows, one could not really walk around the room because it was obvious you were not working, and everything was computerized. The workplace was designed to be non-stimulating, and some employees did not do well, including myself. In September of 2000 I left Blue Cross Blue Shield, and it was more of a mutual parting. I really desired to get back into a clinical setting or at least direct services for health education. I applied for a job with the South Carolina Office on Aging to provide health promotion to senior centers around the state. I thought, finally, I would get out of a corporate office and back to direct services for seniors with face-to-face interactions.

The South Carolina Office on Aging 2002- 2003

The Office on Aging, located in Columbia, SC is the Headquarters for the Senior Centers in South Carolina which offer a variety of services to include home delivered meals and a variety of programs for senior citizens. My job with the Office on Aging was composed of two parts: (1) developing health promotion programs in the senior centers and (2) review the nutrition menus and inspecting the kitchen facilities for proper food storage, cleanliness, and general food safety. It was a dual role for which I had mixed reactions and feelings. I had plenty of flexibility when developing the Health Promotion programs which usually involved healthy eating and exercise, two of my favorite subjects. However, inspecting facilities and reviewing budgets for food expenditures was not exactly my cup of tea and here again is the conundrum facing health educators. While I viewed my job as primarily Health Promotion, my supervisor viewed my job as primarily inspecting Senior Centers for home delivered meals with Health Promotion on the side, so to speak. A long story made short; this job lasted exactly one year. I could at least count the one year towards my retirement with the State of South Carolina.

Chapter 15

Brief Returns to the Family Health Center and SC Department of Health 2002 - 2005

As stated previously, Health Education positions are usually tied to different public health programs (funding sources) which come and go and are time limited. If a health care organization has a position open, even with time limited funding, they post the position anyway or else they are required to return the money to the funder. And so it came to pass that the Family Health Center had a time limited nine-month grant position as a diabetic educator in 2003 and I accepted the position thinking they would "find" the money" to keep me on as a regular health educator. A long story made short, the funding ran out after nine months and I was out of a job! And that was that! Nonetheless, I appreciated the opportunity to work with some of my former co-workers at the Family Health Center, maintain my patient education skills in the general medicine clinic, receive a regular salary with health benefits and pay into a 401k retirement plan, at least temporarily. Again, this is the conundrum of the public health educator who usually has no control over salaries and funding sources. The only hope I had was writing a grant for the Family Health Center which would include a salary for the Health Educator. I wrote several smaller grants and sent them to pharmaceutical companies; however, none were approved. I can honestly say that I was disappointed that the Family Health Center could not find the money to keep me on as a patient educator. There was more than enough work with patients in the general medicine clinic for the other presently employed Health Educator and me, not to mention the need for patient education in the OB-GYN Clinic and community health education. The other Health Educator at the Family Health Center had her PhD in Health

Education and was a friend of mine and I think she felt bad that I had to leave. This meant she had to provide patient education for the general medicine clinic herself without any help.

Luckily for me, I had kept in touch with my friends at the Orangeburg County Health Department and Ryan White Clinic. I resumed patient education during the Thursday night clinic and eventually was offered a full-time position doing AIDS Education and testing in the community. The AIDS testing consisted of using the new saliva testing method. Very few positive results were found using this method. I continued with AIDS Education and testing until 2006 when Hope Health, Inc offered me a position as a Case Manager which included the Ryan White Medical Clinic one night per week.

Chapter 16 -

Hope Health, Inc – 2006 – 2009

The Ryan White Clinic was in the process of transitioning from the Edisto Health District's Orangeburg County Health Department to Hope Health, Inc in 2006. Hope Health, Inc. had a position open as a case manager. While this position enabled me, partially, to return to my passion of clinic-based health education, the case manager position was more like a social worker which required assisting patients trying to get disability, food stamps, Medicaid, prescription drugs and an array of other social services. Looking back and in a way, I accepted the case management position as a favor for the CEO, Carl Humphries, who was the social worker for the Orangeburg Ryan White Clinic. I could have continued my position with the South Carolina Department of Health doing community education and AIDS testing and added those years to my State Retirement plan, however I accepted the Case Manager position with Hope Health, Inc. and worked in this position for three years.

While working for Hope Health, Inc., I could see a continuing problem of our health care system in the United States. All patients attending the Ryan White Clinic, now with Hope Health, Inc., were HIV positive and had an array of other medical problems in addition to AIDS. The Ryan White Clinic, now operating outside of the Health Department walls, conducted the weekly medical clinic with one infectious disease physician. Except for a few patients, none had health insurance and therefore the problem of referrals became evident once again just like patients at the Family Health Center, Inc. If a Ryan White patient needed to see a cardiologist, urologist, or other medical specialist, it was next to impossible to do so. While this was a case manager position, I still had opportunity for patient education, however that was not in my job description and technically, I was not a health educator, I was a case manager. While working for Hope Health, Inc., a new building was being renovated across the street from the Hope Health Office (near the Health Department) in Orangeburg which was to become a Free Medical Clinic called the Orangeburg-Calhoun Free Medical Clinic. This may have been Providential as it opened a whole new aspect of my career in public health. In the back of my mind, I always wanted to work in a Free Medical Clinic. I made the move from Hope Health, Inc to the Orangeburg-Calhoun Free Medical Clinic for a small salary coming from a Blue Cross Blue Shield community health grant. Hope Health, Inc. continued expansion of their organization under the leadership of Carl Humphries to include a clinic in Aiken, SC and a Community Health Center in Florence, South Carolina.

Hope-Health, Inc. today in Orangeburg, South Carolina

Chapter 17 -

The Wonderful World of Non-Profits – 2009 - 2024

As the reader can surmise, public health is a little different from the "for profit" world of private enterprise and corporations like Amazon, and the local "mom and pop" grocery stores. The non-profit world is different. Most non-profits are mission oriented and have a specific service to offer the community. Given the difficulties of finding permanent employment as a public health educator, I decided to form my own non-profit organization in 2006 called Health Education Consultants and applied for recognition with the South Carolina Secretary of State. The application was approved and my organization, Health Education Consultants, became a legitimate 501c non-profit operating legally in the State of South Carolina, hence, Health Education Consultants, Inc. (incorporated). About the same time, in August 2009, as mentioned previously, a Free Medical Clinic was opening across the street from the Hope Health, Inc. office in Orangeburg where I was finishing up my third year of employment. The Orangeburg-Calhoun Free Medical Clinic was a medical clinic as opposed to Hope Health, Inc which was primarily case management/social work with medical clinic one night a week. I decided this would be a good time to "jump ship" and get involved with the Free Medical Clinic and get back to patient education which was my true calling. My involvement with the South Carolina Free Medical Clinics in 2009 lasted for the rest of my career.

The Orangeburg-Calhoun Free Medical Clinic – 2009 – 2012

The Free Medical Clinic in Orangeburg opened its' doors with fanfare, pictures in the local newspaper and a line of indigent patients seeking medical care at the front door of the clinic. None of the patients had medical insurance of any kind to include Medicaid, Medicare, or private insurance. As a matter of fact, the criteria for admission to the clinic was having no insurance of any kind and living at or below the Federal poverty level. There was an abundance of patients with diabetes, high blood pressure, were overweight and smokers; all in my area of interest and expertise. I was glad to further my secondary interest in chronic disease prevention and education. The issue of salary kept coming up and I was able to write a couple of grants successfully and receive a small salary, at least to pay the bills! Sandi Chaplin, RN was the Executive Director of the Free Clinic and basically organized the staff, clinic protocols, fundraising, and even painted the building (inside) which was located next to the Orangeburg County Health Department.

Dr. Bert Gue (pronounced "gay"), who had just retired as a physician in Orangeburg, was the medical director along with Dr. Bernie Johnson who was in the process of retiring. As of this writing, both have passed away within the past three years. Dr. Gue was originally from Orangeburg, talked with a full Southern accent and had an easy demeanor about him, especially since he was recently retired. We got along well except for one conversation about baseball. Being from New Jersey, one could choose between rooting for the Philadelphia Phillies (if you lived in South Jersey) or the New York Yankees if you lived in north Jersey. I aways thought one would root for the home team closest to where you lived. If you lived in South Carolina, you rooted for the Atlanta Braves which was the nearest major league baseball team. Well, Dr. Gue said he was a New York Yankee fan and I asked him how that would be if he was from

South Carolina. I think he was a little offended by that and pointed out the starting center field player for the New York Yankees, Brett Gardner, was from Holly Hill, SC! Nonetheless, Dr. Gue was a Yankee fan from South Carolina!

Dr. Bert Gue

The Orangeburg-Calhoun Free Medical Clinic is a 501c (3) non-profit organization and has a Board of Directors to include local businesspeople, a pastor, educators, a hospital administrator, a banker, and a few other community leaders. The clinic was open three days per week and was staffed by local volunteer physicians, nurses, and administrative volunteers. I was the patient educator and received referrals from physicians. Almost every patient had one of the chronic diseases! I used the same patient education tools from the Family Health Center which came in handy.

As the clinic's only patient educator, I had plenty of work to do with assessments, diabetes education, nutrition, and smoking cessation classes. We had a young lady, Tracy Byrd, who gave us computer support; another woman who was a medical records transcriber; and there were administrative staff, and volunteers. It was a rather close-knit group who had a common purpose: providing medical and health services to patients who had no insurance and who were living at or below the federal poverty level. Another problem area for the health educator and staff was medications. Usually, patients conclude the doctor's visit with a handful of prescriptions and no money to buy the medications. The patient educator's job is to teach patients the purpose of medications and how to take them. This was a difficult job because it was not unusual for patients to be on multiple medications for a variety of reasons. Prescription medications were a challenge for physicians as they tried to prescribe the generic medications, however sometimes there were brand name only which necessitated the patient assistance program application. In 2009, patient assistance applications to pharmaceutical companies were still on paper which required duplicate copies, signatures and other detailed information and then mailed into the pharmaceutical companies. This process could take weeks for the medications to arrive safely in the mail. These were the challenges for the physicians, nurses, patient educators, and administrative staff. For the most part, today, patient assistance programs for medications are computerized and patients can get their medications in a timely manner.

While the clinic provided excellent primary care and health education, there was always the problem of referrals, like the Family Health Center and the Ryan White Clinic, only in the Free Medical Clinic, the problem seemed more acute. Since there was no established referral system in place, the doctors at the Free Clinic had to rely on their friends who were physicians and who would see a patient for free. While this might work a few times, doctors are hesitant to see a patient for free fearing a floodgate of referrals and then lost revenue to pay their own staff. This "problem" persists throughout the South Carolina Free Medical Clinics today, especially those clinics located in the rural areas of the State. In my opinion, this further enhanced the importance of health education, especially among chronic diseases. If you prevent or delay the progression of chronic diseases, then the need for referrals would not be as great. When I provided patient education at the clinic, I saw patients with heart disease who were quite young, were heavy smokers and/or heavy drinkers of alcoholic beverages. Some patients had kidney disease due to diabetes, some had strokes or partial strokes due to persistent hypertension, some had emphysema and lung disease due to cigarette smoking and some patients were just obese and suffered from bone, hip, knee, and ankle injuries. As I have always said, there was a no shortage of work for the patient educator: as "the harvest is great, and the laborers are few."

As I provided the patient education, I was learning about the operations of a non-profit organization. A non-profit clinic had to be constantly "looking" for money in the form of grants, fundraising and asking for donations. I was not accustomed to these additional duties, other than occasional grant writing. If I wanted a salary, I had to participate in the fundraising, as did everyone else including the physicians! I learned that other non-profit organizations do the same thing: grants, fundraise, and seek donations. I was a reluctant participant. When I worked for the State of South Carolina, I was paid every two weeks and I could concentrate on my work (and not worry about a paycheck), when I worked for the Family Health Center, I was paid every two weeks and not have to worry about a paycheck and the same for Hope Health, Inc. However, with non-profits I had to concentrate on my work, or mission if you will, **and** do the fundraising, grant writing, and ask for donations, if I wanted to be paid a salary! This is the wonderful world of non-profits! As it turns out, most 501c3 nonprofits are run this way. At Christmas time, 2009, we sold wreaths and had a fundraising party at the local community college. Dr. Gue's wife, Jeanne Gue, was kind enough to mail out fundraising letters and call potential donors on the phone.

I learned a lot at the Orangeburg-Calhoun Free Medical Clinic both as a patient educator and the general operations of a non-profit organization. The South Carolina Free Clinic Association is in Camden, South Carolina and there are some 15 other Free Clinics around the State, some are large clinics, and some are small. All the Free Clinics are 501c3 nonprofits; some are associated with local churches, food pantries, homeless shelters, or another social services agency. All are unique in way, reflecting the culture of the community. For the most part, the admission criteria are the same: having no medical insurance and living at or below the federal poverty level (usually food stamp level). Since the patients do not have health insurance, there is no billing and hence, no revenue or income coming into the clinic, therefore going back to grants, fundraising, and seeking donations. The South Carolina Department of Health receives funding from the State legislature each year, community health centers receive some federal funding. However, the South Carolina Free Clinics do not receive any of this funding, at least not in any appreciable amount.

From a Free Medical Clinic perspective, I could see the plight of the uninsured person who did not have access to medical care, not just in Orangeburg, SC, however in the United States as well. There is always the Emergency Room at the local hospital, however that is only band aid treatment, not primary or specialty care.

In Orangeburg, there was community support for the Free Clinic. The local pharmacy worked with the clinic to get as many generic medications as possible; a local food pantry call "Compassion in Action" provided food for the patients; the Samaritan House helped with housing; the Baptist Church provided pastoral counseling and so forth. However, after three years, I decided to move on to another larger clinic in Columbia, SC called the Columbia Free Medical Clinic which offered medical services five days per week, Monday through Friday and offered an array of specialty services for Free Clinic patients.

It should be noted, the Orangeburg Regional Medical Hospital provided support for lab services and helped with grants and funding. The late Brenda Williams was instrumental with facilitating the lab services and diagnostic examinations as well. She was also the Chairperson of the Board of Directors. The Orangeburg-Calhoun Free Medical Clinic continues in operation today offering basic primary care services on certain days of the week.

Stories from the Field – Plight of the Uninsured Patient

> I will never forget a lady who came into the clinic with her husband, and who was just discharged from the Regional Medical Center in Orangeburg for heart disease. She was in her mid to late 50's and still had her hospital wristband on. She was instructed by her attending physician at the hospital, upon discharge, to see her family doctor for follow-up medical care. As it turned out, she was from neighboring Bamberg County and was not eligible for services at the Orangeburg-Calhoun Free Medical Clinic, so we had to turn her away. She didn't have a family physician as she could not afford one. I often wondered what ever happened to her as I knew there were very few physicians in Bamberg County and even if there were enough physicians, they would probably not see her because she had no medical insurance, thus the plight of the uninsured patient.

Orangeburg-Calhoun Free Medical Clinic in 2009

Orangeburg-Calhoun Free Medical Clinic Today on Doyle St.

Chapter 18 -

Columbia Free Medical Clinic – 2012 -2014

In 2012, I made the leap from a start-up Free Medical Clinic in Orangeburg to the Columbia Free Medical Clinic which had been in operation for 30 years, offered a full range of medical services Monday through Friday and had an established specialty referral network. Columbia is the state capitol of South Carolina with some 3 million residents, the University of South Carolina, Fort Jackson Military base and several other colleges and technical schools. The Columbia Free Medical clinic had ample volunteer physicians, nurse practitioners, nurses, and general medical personnel. The University of South Carolina has schools of medicine, pharmacy, nursing, public health, and the allied health professions. These schools were constantly looking for opportunities for their students to practice their chosen profession in the form of a practicum, placement, or community service. In addition, there were doctors who were retired or semi-retired who wanted to keep their medical license active. Admission to the Columbia Free Medical Clinic is generally the same as other Free Clinics throughout the state: (1) have no health insurance of any kind and (2) living at or below the federal poverty level (food stamp level of income). The Columbia Free Medical Clinic had an "inhouse" pharmacy which was quite a benefit for patients attending this clinic. The clinic opened around 7am, however patients began lining up by 6am for services on a "first come, first serve basis." When I arrived in 2012, there was no patient educator on staff. The CEO, Dennis Coker, was a retired military officer and since I was also retired from the military, we seemed to work together quite well. The clinic had seven or eight exam rooms, and patients were admitted to the clinic early in the morning. There was considerable lag time between when the patient was placed in an exam room and when the physician or nurse practitioner arrived to see the patients: usually about 30 minutes or more as the physician worked his or her way from room to room. Thirty minutes was ample time for me to perform health education assessments and talk with patients about their health. Almost every patient had some chronic disease beginning with diabetes and hypertension. There was more than enough work for this patient educator to do. Thankfully, I had students from the University of South Carolina helping me, who were very energetic, and willing to help!

As I eased into my new job, I had to become familiar with the patient populations who attended the Columbia Free Medical Clinic. There was a huge homeless population in Columbia, and they were among the first to sign up for services outside the clinic at 6am. One could always recognize the homeless person as they were usually carrying a large backpack with them which contained their worldly belongings. To my amazement many of the homeless patients seem overweight! When I shared this observation with one of my co-workers, he said that is because they eat only one meal per day at a soup kitchen or homeless shelter; they (the homeless person), would overeat or stuff themselves because that would be their only meal for the day. Usually, that one meal would be loaded with starches such as corn, potatoes, bread, lima beans, and pasta etc., thus running the risk of obesity and diabetes. I could see this was going to be a challenging job! In addition to the homeless, we had patients from India, China or Taiwan, Africa, and Mexico. It was easy to get into the Columbia Free Medical Clinic as there was no residency requirement, in other words, a patient could be from another country or another county in South Carolina and still be admitted to the clinic if he/she had no health insurance.

During the first year there were some 600 individual patient education encounters and in addition, there were weekly group health education classes which averaged eight to ten participants. Usually, the participants already received individual patient education and the group class would reinforce concepts which were taught individually. All encounters with the patient, whether individual or group, were documented in the patient's medical record. I submitted a monthly report to the CEO which was used in grant writing for the clinic. It was at this time at the Columbia Free Medical Clinic that Patient Education was established as part of the healthcare team along with the physician, pharmacist, registered nurse, medical assistant, and others. Patient education became part of the patient "flow" as the patient went from one station to another in the clinic. Usually, patient education occurred either while the patient was waiting for the physician in the exam room or when the physician finished with the physician and on his or her way to the pharmacy. This was another challenge for the patient educator in a clinic setting: getting the referral from the physician or Nurse Practitioner and staying within the patient flow. My goal was to make the Patient Educator part of the healthcare team.

Some of the patients could not read or write, so we had to use special educational materials for them and use audio-visuals such as PowerPoint and You-Tube from the internet on a projector and screen in the classroom. Patient Education at the Columbia Free Medical Clinic presented many challenges: the patient population was diverse (different ethnic groups), a transient population including the homeless, literacy challenges with limited formal schooling, and transportation as many patients had no cars and had to rely on others to get to the clinic. In a way, the patient educator had a "one shot" opportunity for health education as the patient may or may not be returning to the clinic for a variety of reasons.

While working at the Columbia Free Medical Clinic furthered my career as a professional health educator, I could simultaneously see the continued plight of the uninsured patient population. The Columbia Free Clinic had a nice system of referrals, at least on paper. However, I often wondered how well the system of referrals was working for specialty care as patients were often lost to follow-up. Transportation was always a problem. The clinic received a large sum of money in the form of a grant for patients to call a taxi to keep their appointments. Problems would arise where a taxi would arrive at the address given, however the driver could not find the patient at home and so forth. This is not the fault of the clinic; it is just the transitory nature of the patient population and their ability to keep appointments for a variety of reasons. After a while, the specialty physicians would stop seeing Free Clinic patients because the specialty physician would lose money since they gave up a slot or appointment which would go unfilled, hence lost revenue.

The Columbia Free Medical Clinic provided ample experience to practice my profession. We averaged around 600 patient encounters per year, for three consecutive years. The weekly group classes were well attended. Nursing students gave presentations, pre-medical students collected data for input into the Excel computer system to keep track of the patient's progress; public health students "shadowed" me when providing patient education in the clinic exam rooms. Then there were general volunteers such as local teachers who were retired and wanted to help in some way, like collecting educational materials for the patients.

While I was practicing health education at the Columbia Free Medical Clinic, I kept an eye on my newly formed Health Education Consultants, Inc. organization which I formed in 2007. In a way, the organization was dormant as I was busy with the clinic work in Orangeburg and Columbia. While working at the Columbia clinic, I managed to find time to apply for a 501c (3) non-profit status with the Internal Revenue Service. While Health Education Consultants, Inc. was recognized by the State of South Carolina., it was not yet recognized as a non-profit organization by the Internal Revenue Service. Recognition by the IRS meant fundraising contributions would be tax deductible, and we could apply for grants, independently from the Free Clinics. I organized a small group of people to become the Board of Directors to include Dr. Kevin McRedmond, Lynda Byers, RN, Dr. Lydia Willingham and Dee Struchen, NP. To my amazement, the IRS approved our application, and they sent us a letter of recognition in November of 2014 as an official 501c (3) organization! By January of 2015, I was ready to move on to the Newberry Free Medical Clinic and the Good Samaritan Clinics in Columbia which was a primarily Spanish speaking patient population. Working in these two clinics will take us to 2024 where Health Education Consultants, Inc. still provides patient education, though on a limited basis.

The Columbia Free Medical Clinic today on Harden Street in Columbia, South Carolina.

We received our 501c (3) recognition from the Internal Revenue Service in November 2014.

MISSION STATEMENT

Health Education Consultants, Inc.

The Mission of Health Education Consultants is to alleviate the suffering and prevent or delay the onset of chronic diseases such as obesity, diabetes, hypertension, heart disease among medically underserved and uninsured populations in South Carolina through health education, wellness, and changes in lifestyle.

VISION STATEMENT

To have a healthy South Carolina population through health promotion and education exemplified by voluntary behavior change in nutrition, exercise, smoking cessation, and the management of chronic diseases.

Dave graduates from the South Carolina Non-Profit Institute 2014

(Dave is second from left to right)

Chapter 19

Newberry Free Medical Clinic -2015 – Present

The Newberry Free Medical Clinic is located some 25 miles Northwest of Columbia, SC and is governed by a Board of Directors, a CEO, Ms. Pamela Branton and employ two Certified Medical Assistants. There are two volunteer physicians and a Family Nurse Practitioner who specializes in women's health, specifically, GYN or gynecology. Each physician volunteers one day a week. I am the Patient Educator. The clinic takes care of about 200 uninsured patients. The Newberry Free Medical Clinic is unique in that it serves the residents of Newberry County only. The town of Newberry has a college with an excellent reputation for business and the arts. It has many well-known alumni. There is some manufacturing nearby, along with Amick chicken farms and a lumber mill. The Newberry County Memorial Hospital is a medium size hospital serving the community. There are a handful of physicians having offices nearby. The Newberry Free Clinic is located across the street from the hospital.

Admission to the Newberry Free Medical clinic consists of: (1) proof of residency in Newbery County; (2) a picture ID card; (3) proof of income and (3) a social security card. As I began my health education assessments, I noticed that most of the patients have never lived outside of Newberry County, had limited formal education (many do not have high school diplomas), their employment history was rather sketchy with on and off jobs, and their overall health was not good. By this, I mean there were patients coming to the clinic who were in their late 40's and early 50's and have already experienced a stroke due to hypertension and diabetes and they have a host of other chronic diseases. Some were applying for disability at a very young age. In a way, Newberry was a microcosm for the rest of South Carolina with the high incidence of chronic diseases. Patients who worked at the Amick Farms chicken processing plant and the lumber mill had work related health problems especially for repetitious movement of the shoulders and arms while working on a conveyer belt. Patients would come in with rotor cuff and elbow injuries and thus applying for disability.

The Newberry Free Medical Clinic is a little more "manageable" than the larger Free Medical Clinic in Columbia. There are six exam rooms, and I am able to work around the doctors for patient education. Some of the patients are very interested in improving their health, some patients not so much, and then others really didn't care one way or another. I am careful not to spend too much time with those who didn't care to improve their health to conserve my energy. Most women seemed to be interested in losing weight. It is not unusual for see female patients weighing more than 200 pounds. With obesity comes the associated risks of knee, ankle, and hip problems not to mention diabetes and hypertension.

As mentioned earlier in this book, the remedy for many of these chronic diseases revolve around the triad of nutrition, exercise, and medication. These are simple concepts however they are rather elusive and require behavior change which is hard to do for most people. For nutrition, we use the food pyramid which is taught in health classes in grammar and high school. Exercise is an aerobic activity for 20 – 30 minutes five days per week. Brisk walking would count or any activity to increase the heart rate. Medications are the last resort if nutrition and exercise do not work. However, many patients want to skip the meal plan and exercise and go straight to the medications or pills, it's easier. The problem here is that if a certain dose of medication does not work, the healthcare provider will increase the dose, and perhaps add another pill. After a while, a patient will walk into the clinic with a Walmart bag full of pills! And most pills have side effects. As I mentioned earlier, in a facetious way, I have always said the doctors have the easy job of just prescribing the medicine and say come back in two weeks while the patient educator must work on behavior change which is much harder to do (compared to prescribing the mediations).

It was at the Newberry Free Medical Clinic that Health Education Consultants, Inc. formalized the placement of college students into a practicum for pre-medical students (now Exercise Science), nursing, public health, future Nurse Practitioners and Physician Assistants. My goal was to expose the students to the plight of the uninsured patients who were poor, according to Federal poverty guidelines, and who had few resources, not even a car. The placement of students into the Newberry Free Medical Clinic required documentation in the form of a MOA (Memorandum of Agreement) between Health Education Consultants, Inc., and the University of South Carolina School of Public Health. The MOA is a four-page legal document requiring signatures from both parties which describes obligations for safety of the students, general hours of work in the clinic, evaluation of the students at the end of the practicum and general conduct in the clinic. The following is a typical job description for students performing a practicum with Health Education Consultants, Inc:

Health Education Consultants, Inc.

Student Practicum

Health Education Consultants, Inc. facilitates behavior change for patients attending South Carolina Free Medical Clinics and provides health education to alleviate the suffering and prevent or delay the onset of chronic diseases including obesity, diabetes, and high blood pressure among uninsured populations in South Carolina and those who live at or below Federal poverty guidelines.

The Student Practicum is designed to familiarize the student with the day-to-day operation of the Free Medical Clinics of South Carolina; provide one-on-one encounters with patients who have chronic illness; and facilitate behavior change to improve their personal health.

Students will:

- Work as team members among clinic staff including physicians, nurses, pharmacists, medical assistants, and volunteers.
- Perform patient assessment of health literacy and health knowledge; develop an education intervention plan; and document patient-centered behavior goals.
- Evaluate the behavioral health improvement e.g., nutritional changes, exercise frequency and duration at the next patient visit either in person or via tele-health.
- Document the assessment, intervention and evaluation in the patient medical record either written or electronically.
- "Shadow" an experienced professional health educator in the clinic setting, take notes, make observations, provide feedback related to the patient interaction and offer suggestions for personal health improvement.
- Spend 15 -20 hours per week and keep a journal of clinical activities.
- Participate in grant writing for Health Education Consultants, Inc.
- Participate in writing policies and procedures related to patient education in a clinic setting.
- Research and develop educational materials related to the literacy/educational level of patients;
- Initiate and participate in community fundraising events.
- Wear clothing appropriate for work in a professional health care setting.

Rev. March 2, 2021

Patient Education progressed very well at the Newberry Free Medical clinic as I developed an Excel database to track patients with their vital signs, glucose, weight, blood pressure, cholesterol, and other health indicators. We had several patients who quit smoking after I talked to them about the benefits of being smoke free, not to mention the money saved. We documented everything as that was what the nurses taught me throughout my career (if it wasn't documented, it wasn't done!) As our success continued, we were able to get a small grant from Aflac Insurance Company to help pay for educational materials, our website, and help pay for travel expenses. We developed a Facebook page and posted patient testimonies or success stories which helped with fundraising and getting donations. We had a 5k run at Dreher Island, though not well attended (it was the first time), however we raised money from those who said they couldn't run but gave a twenty-dollar donation. Health Education Consultants, Inc. was growing nicely: seeing clinic patients on a regular basis in a systematic fashion, formalizing practicum agreements with the University of South Carolina and most importantly, facilitating behavior change among the patients.

Probably the most challenging job a patient educator encounters, is proving that health education works or as academics would call it "efficacy of health education." This is where the study of epidemiology and data collection comes in handy. One looks for a decrease in emergency room visits from chronic diseases; a decrease in hospital admissions, decrease use of dialysis centers and other indicators. Sometimes, it will take several years for these indicators to appear which is why it is important to document behavior change and health improvements during patient encounters.

I would be amiss if I did not mention the two medical assistants at the Newberry Free Medical Clinic: Cynthia Wallace and Lesa Taylor. Both are strong Christians and care for every patient coming through the front door of the clinic. Cynthia Wallace is a former school bus driver and decided to return to the local technical school to get her medical assistant certification after 26 years of bus driving for the Newberry School District. I like to say she "runs a tight ship" with attention to detail. I really came to appreciate her as the Covid19 broke loose and we had to wear face protection, keep six feet apart and observe all CDC (Centers for Disease Control) protocols and guidelines. We had several patients with Covid19 who attended the Newberry Free Medical Clinic. Cynthia knows all the patients from Newberry and their family members as well. She is a good listener while performing vital signs and charting their medication list. Both Cynthia and Lesa take a personal and a Christian approach to helping patients. Patients feel loved and cared for at the Newberry Clinic. They look after the patients as if they were family members. Cynthia and Lesa also supervise medical assistant students who come through the clinic from the local technical school and Newberry College. They become part of the family also.

Stories from the field – Covid19 Epidemic in South Carolina, March 2019

When the Covid19 pandemic began in 2019, Health Education Consultants focused on chronic disease prevention and education. However, as the pandemic worsened, we had to change our mission to Covid19 prevention and education. I was supervising three University of South Carolina students at the time, and we revised our patient education aligning with the Center for Disease Control guidelines: wearing face protection, social distancing, educating patients about the signs and symptoms of Covid19, travel restrictions, infection control within the clinic setting, frequent washing of hands for both patients and staff and patient education to keep the immune system strong to resist viral infection. We added a nutrition component to our patient education with an emphasis on proteins, vitamins, and minerals. We stressed the importance of exercising to keep the immune system strong. Our efforts did not go unnoticed as a national newsletter for public health education wrote an article about how Covid19 affected our mission and how we had to change our mission to prevent the transmission of Covid19 in the clinic and the community as well. While a national "newsletter" may not be the same as a Harvard Medical journal or Johns Hopkins journal, it is nice to be recognized by our peers. A copy of the article may be found in Appendix 3.

Stories from the Field – Bank Robbery in Whitmire, South Carolina (some time ago)

As told by Lesa Taylor, Medical Assistant

Lesa Taylor is from a little town call Whitmire, SC where apparently everyone knows everyone not unlike Mayberry R.F.D. There is one traffic light, one or two general stores, a bank, a police station, and a gas station. As the story goes, there was a bank robbery one day, apparently during lunch hour when many of the bank employees were out for lunch. The police station was right next door to the bank and there was only one deputy on duty with his feet up on his desk. The deputy did not hear a thing and the robber made a clean getaway, probably without too much money! Lesa has plenty of stories to tell like this.

Lesa Taylor   Pam Branton, CEO, and Cynthia Wallace

Chapter 20 -

Good Samaritan Clinics – 2015 – 2023

The Good Samaritan Clinic is headquartered in Columbia, SC with branch clinics in Chapin, Edisto Island and West Columbia. Since there is more than one clinic, the plural is used, hence, Good Samaritan Clinics. The Columbia Clinics are primarily for Spanish speaking patients; however, the clinics are open to anyone without health insurance. The Good Samaritan Clinics have Spanish interpreters on site who are frequently students from Spanish speaking countries. These clinics are unique to Health Education Consultants, Inc. in that interpreters are provided to health educators when patient education is given for diabetes, hypertension, cholesterol, smoking cessation, and the other chronic diseases. Therefore, the patient education was a three-way conversation between the Health Education practitioner, the patient and interpreter. I always appreciated the Good Samaritan clinic's support for health education, as it was valued enough that an interpreter would be provided.

Health Education for the Spanish population has unique challenges besides the language barrier. Health Educational materials must be translated, easy to understand and culturally sensitive. I always found working with the Spanish population quite enjoyable. Without stereotyping, most Hispanics attending the clinics are easygoing, like to listen to music, are very courteous, appreciative of services offered by the clinic, and eager to learn. Hispanics are hardworking with men working in construction or labor jobs while women have domestic jobs like housecleaning or working in motels. Most of the patients are from Mexico and Central America: Honduras, Guatemala, Costa Rica, and Nicaragua. The Percival Road Clinic director, Dr. Lidia Navarrete, is from El Salvador.

When providing patient education to the Spanish population, we focus on the traditional chronic diseases, just like the other clinics. We might ask general questions like: what country are you from? However, we don't ask questions about citizenship, documentation, immigration, green cards, work visas and the like, unless the patient wishes to discuss those topics. For all I know, the patients could have driven their cars across the Mexican border to Texas and onto South Carolina. Admission to the Good Samaritan clinics does not require proof of residence or proof of income. It is open admission. There are volunteer doctors, nurses, and other administrative staff associated with the University of South Carolina Medical School who help provide health services and some social services such as teaching the Spanish patients how to read and speak English.

The Good Samaritan Clinic in Chapin, SC is a satellite clinic located in Chapin, SC which is next to Lake Murry and is home to a large retiree population. This is good news for the Chapin clinic director as there are many retirees who are former doctors, nurses, administrative personnel, and other allied health. In fact, there are more volunteers than patients on most given clinic nights. Chapin is the smallest clinic served by Health Education Consultants, Inc., meets one time per week, and averages 5 or 6 patients per clinic; some are appointments, and some are "walk-ins." The challenge for health educators working in a small clinic is the same as the larger clinics, that is, performing the patient education before the patient leaves the clinic. Most of the time, patient education can be performed while the patient is in clinic, however on occasion, an appointment will be made for a return visit. As with the other clinics, all health education is documented in the medical records, some on paper, some on the laptop computer. Again, the goal is behavior change, health improvements with blood pressure, diabetes/blood sugar/glucose control weight reduction, smoking cessation and general health and well-being. An additional note on the Good Samaritan Clinic/Chapin is that it is a church-based organization affiliated with the local Methodist Church. They view the clinic as a ministry of the church as well as a medical service to the community. Also, many of the volunteer's "minister" to each other concerning their personal health problems and other needs. I always view the Chapin Clinic as the "fun" clinic since the volunteers are so upbeat, motivated to help others, offer encouragement, and support and keep the atmosphere of the clinic "light" so to speak. The Chapin Clinic director, Sue Boland, keeps everyone on task and looks to the needs of volunteers and patients. Please see below a nice patient testimony from Karen Deleon who was a patient from the Good Samaritan Clinic on Old Percival Road from a few years ago.

Stories from the Field – Karen Deleon, Age 31, Patient at Good Samaritan Clinic

I have been coming to the Good Samaritan Clinic on Percival Road for five years. I attended a health fair sponsored by the Good Samaritan Clinic in 2016 and was in good health at the time. I started having some heart palpitations. The Clinic checked my thyroid, and it was normal. At the same time, I was getting concerned about my blood pressure, my heart, and possible diabetes which runs in my family on my mother's side. My weight was 239 pounds, and I am 5'2". I talked with Mr. Dave about a meal plan to lose weight. He used a Spanish meal plan for around 1600 calories. I found it difficult to plan meals with the Spanish food, especially snacks such as Pina colada (a pineapple with peanuts), sweet salsa, chicharrons, tortes and other bakery items including bread. Also, we eat a lot of beans and rice which affects my weight and overall health. I decided to make some changes. What I was eating was killing me. I decided to take seriously my health and my family. I did some research on diabetes and recognized the foods which cause diabetes, mainly sweets and starches. I followed the meal plan and now weigh 189 pounds. At first it was difficult; however, I am more disciplined now that I know what to eat. I walk as much as I can. I use a pedometer and walk at least 3,000 steps per day which burns a lot of calories.

I do not take any medications for diabetes or high blood pressure. I cook healthily for my husband and two children, and they are much healthier now. I found out it is cheaper to be healthy. I think the other patients who attend the Good Samaritan Clinic should get informed and make healthy food choices to improve their overall health and avoid diseases such as high blood pressure and diabetes. It does not cost money to exercise. You can walk around the parks and shopping areas. It is necessary to walk until you sweat or perspire. I am thankful for the help I found at the Good Samaritan Clinic. Finally, I pray to God for letting me live a long life and be healthy. And for my family too!

Chapter 21

Culture in a Public Health Education Career

When I was beginning my first professional job in public health, a co-work told me that every organization has a certain "culture." To move up in the organization and work well within the organization, I must be mindful of the culture. Here is a general review of the culture of the organizations I worked with in this book. I will try my best not to stereotype! Please keep in mind that I am from New Jersey and raised on the Eastern seaboard with Philadelphia across the river and New York City to the North, so I am very much a middle Atlantic sort of guy.

My first professional job was with the West Virginia Department of Health in Charleston, West Virginia. The stereotype of West Virginia of course is the hillbilly, mountains, poverty etc. As it turns out, the person who hired me was Bob Anderson who was from upstate New York (a Yankee if you will), the person who referred me to the state position in South Carolina was Jennifer Long, my classmate who is from Cumberland, Maryland, another East Coast state; my immediate supervisor at the West Virgina Department of Health, Dr. Richard Hopkins was from Ohio, however he went to medical school in Philadelphia, Pennsylvania, so we had lots of discussions about Philadelphia; the other physician epidemiologist in the West Virgina state office was Dr. Roy Baron who was from New York City; the person in charge of the hemophilia program (getting factor 8 to patients) was a woman named Lynn (I forgot her last name) was from North Jersey; and there were two other employees at the state office who were from West Virginia. I say all of this because the pre-dominant culture at the state office for the AIDS program was middle Atlantic, white, highly educated people. I seemed to fit right in. While this may seem to be a generalization of culture, it is something to consider especially as you follow this narrative.

My second professional job was with the <u>South Carolina Department of Health</u> and as I mentioned earlier, this was the deep South. Anyway, the dominant culture at the Orangeburg County Health Department (Edisto Health District) was white, female nurses. Well, that didn't seem like a big deal and on a facetious note, there were so many of them on every floor of the building! I enjoyed their Southern accents and all of attention they gave me coming from the North and I was one the few men on staff at the Health Department. The point here is that the dominant culture here was white, female, Southern culture, and nurses. They all respected my professional degree and skills however I always got the feeling I was "their health educator." It wasn't really a big deal as I learned to work around that as we all had common interests with the welfare of the patients and clients using the health department services.

My third professional organization was the <u>Family Health Centers, Inc</u> in Orangeburg. When starting work there in October 1996, I was one of four white men working in the building. The Family Health Centers is a predominately black organization, so I was obviously in the minority. There were a few other white nurses working there also. I was always appreciative of the staff at the Family Health Center who addressed me as Mr. Brangan, a sign of respect. Most realized I was there to serve the patients in the clinic regardless of race, creed, or color. So, the dominant culture here is African American staff and patient/clients were mostly African American also. It was just something to keep in mind when performing my health education duties and working with staff.

My fourth professional organization was Hope-Health, Inc in Orangeburg. Though I knew the CEO, I didn't know the other staff members who worked at the main office in Florence and Aiken, SC. To make a long story short, Hope Health's predominant culture was LGBQ. So here we have another culture with different values as myself, nonetheless I went forward to serve the patients and clients. One of the employees at Hope Health said to me, "Dave, I am not sure you fit in here at Hope Health". Another interesting observation during my three-year employment at Hope-Health, Inc. was that I had five co-workers including two supervisors who were divorced, and a sixth co-worker was a young man in his mid-thirties and never been married. I bring this up not to be judgmental, just as an observation. I was the only married man in the Orangeburg Office of Hope-Health, Inc. My supervisor was a divorced female, and her supervisor was a divorced female. The predominant culture at Hope-Health, Inc appeared to be LBGQ and divorced women. Perhaps my co-worker was right when he said "Dave, I don't think you fit in here with this organization."

The fifth organization, <u>the Orangeburg-Calhoun Free Medical Clinic</u>, was a community-based Orangeburg, SC culture. The Board of Directors was composed mostly of local people except one from Ohio and one from New Jersey. The staff members (paid staff and volunteers) were all from the Orangeburg area. It was a Southern culture for sure.

The sixth organization, the Columbia Free Medical Clinic, had more of a cosmopolitan or city culture being the state capital and home to the University of South Carolina. The CEO, Dennis Coker was retired from the military, so we communicated well; the charge nurse was from Albany, New York, the Nurse Practitioner was Dee Struchen, FNP, who received her degree from the University of Pennsylvania at age 52 was from New Jersey. There were numerous preceptors and students performing practicums at the Columbia Free Medical Clinic which created a nice academic atmosphere. However, in the management and Board of Directors, was still the "good old boy" system in place and that was part of the organization culture. If you went to the right school such the University of South Carolina and the right churches, you might move up in the organization.

The seventh organization is the Good Samaritan Clinics which is a church-based organization, thus another culture, a religious one, sponsored by the United Methodist church in Columbia, SC, and the Chapin United Methodist Church. The culture here is caring and compassion for the patients. However, I did notice when I started work at the Good Samaritan Clinics someone asked me: which church do I go to? I go to the Catholic church regularly on Sunday though I wondered what that person would think if I said I didn't go to church

The eighth and last organization is Health Education Consultants, Inc which is a very diverse organization with Board members and students from a variety of backgrounds. Our initial Board of Directors was composed of Doris Drayton, NP who was African American female, Lynda Beyers, RN who was a white nurse from the midwest, Kristi Coleman, RN, African American female, Adam Gause, white male, Alan Yong, Asian American, Lydia Willingham, black female, Paul Zenk, white male, and Wanda Ramos, Hispanic American. So, we have a nice diverse population with Health Education Consultants, Inc.

In summary, I have worked for:

(1) West Virginia Department of Health with a middle Atlantic white male culture at the state capital in Charleston, West Virginia

(2) the South Carolina Department of Health in Orangeburg SC with a white, female, nurse dominant culture.

(3) The Family Health Centers, Inc. with a predominately African American culture

(4) Orangeburg-Calhoun Free Medical Clinic – predominately Southern rural culture

(5) Hope-Health Inc with a predominately LBGBQ and divorced women culture

(6) The Columbia Free Medical Clinic with a cosmopolitan, academic/collegiate culture though the "good old boy" system still in place.

(7) The Good Samaritan Clinics in Columbia and Chapin, SC with the dominant culture being the Presbyterian and Methodist churches.

(8) Health Education Consultants, Inc, - a diverse Board member culture: white male and white female; black female, Hispanic, Asian-American, and African American male students.

Epilog

Public Health Education has come a long way since the early 1980's as exemplified by schools of public health offering professional degrees including master's and PhD. The challenge has always been to show the efficacy of health education, in other words that health education really works. Behavior change is difficult as the Michael Jackson song says, just "look at the man in the mirror." Health education must be "voluntary change in behavior" as defined by Dr. Laurence Green. However difficult, it can be done. In Appendix Two of this book are 20 testimonies from patients, mostly from the Newberry Free Medical Clinic, who have improved their health through nutrition, exercise and proper medication taking. Some have discontinued medication completely! There are other clinic patients who have benefited from patient education though their testimonies have not been collected. Their health improvements have been documented in their medical records. These are simple concepts and health professionals must make the effort at patient education by sitting down with the patient, listening to their concerns, complete health education assessments, and establishing health goals with the patient. The health care provider cannot simply hand the patient a pamphlet and call it patient education.

In addition to seeing patients improve their health and discontinuing medications is the joy of working with students who are completing a practicum with Health Education Consultants, Inc as part of their graduation requirements. Most have come from the University of South Carolina schools of Public Health, Exercise Science, or pre-med studies, however, there have been other schools such as such as Liberty University, Spellman in Atlanta, Georgia, and American University in Washington, DC. They are energetic, eager to learn and enthusiastic about patient education. I learned from the students too! They all have innovative approaches to patient education. The students are applying to medical schools, Physician Assistant schools, nurse practitioner and nursing schools and public health graduate programs. Many needed a letter of recommendation for admission to their selected schools. I write good letters of recommendation and for the most part, the students were admitted to the school of their choice. I like to think that I had a small part in their admission and future success.

As a reminder, in the appendix, I have included several newspaper articles I wrote for the Orangeburg newspaper, "The Times and Democrat" in 2010/11. The articles are about healthcare reform and the healthcare system in the United States, and they are still relevant today. However, the purpose of this book is not to advocate for healthcare reform but to bring to light the "plight" of the uninsured person who cannot get healthcare and invariably die an early and unnecessary death. At the same time, the value of health education increases because the goal is prevention to avoid premature death and morbidity.

Hopefully, in the future, clinic-based patient education will receive additional support in the form of salaries, office space, and recognition as being part of the health care team. Much progress has been made over the past 30 years as exemplified by an interest in health behaviors in healthcare settings. Physicians, registered nurses, nurse practitioners and pharmacists are increasingly giving attention to behavior change (or motivation). Many pharmacists are becoming diabetes educators as well. For now, "the harvest is great, and the laborers are few," however I think we are going in the right direction!

Thanks and Acknowledgements

First, thank you to my wife, Karen, who stood by me as I worked in Public Health with its ups and downs and varied healthcare settings from State level work to grassroots health education. She has been supportive and kept the home fires going. And course my kids, Becky and Tim who wondered what I did all day in public health!

Dr. Lydia Willingham who has been with Health Education Consultants, Inc. since 2014 and has served on the Board of Directors, helped with fundraising, and has supported our mission with dedication and steadfastness. The other Board members are Kevin McRedmond, Adam Gause, Wanda Ramos, Alan Jung (treasurer), and Kristi Coleman. Each one brought a unique and valuable contribution to Health Education Consultants, Inc. And of course, thank you to my friends who have volunteered to proofread, edit, and look for continuity of thought with the manuscript: Teresa Heilman, Carolyn Hartley, and June Cannon.

Volunteers and Students

There have been so many volunteers that it is almost impossible to count them all, however I will try and list as many as I can remember:

Luzma Moody. Spanish translator
Lawanda Canzater (student volunteer)
Mike Martucci
Nicole Royer (USC Practicum)
Mary White
Dee Struchen, FNP
Jean Emenecker, RN
Marie Callahan, RN
Michelle Adams – former Board Member
Linda Byars – former Board Member
Delenna Kessler (student community service)
Paul Zenk – former Board Member
Rayona Benloss – volunteer
Conner Lentz (student community service)
Jessica Campo (student community service)
Brenda DuBoise (student Practicum)
Iris Portee – Free Clinic patient
Ykesha Young – Benedict University student
Doris Drayton – former Board member
Nick Doyle (USC Student Practicum)
Perpetua Bello-Ogunu (Student Practicum)

Aakash Patel (USC Practicum)
Cameron Perkins (USC Practicum)
Riya Gajjar (USC Practicum)
Madison Naulty (USC Practicum)
Jessica Campo – USC Student volunteer
Laila Hussein USC Student Volunteer
Renee Lussier (USC Student Practicum)
Paul Zenk – former Board Member
Robert Tyler – USC Thesis student
Jai McQuilla – Spellman College student
Ruosi Liu – USC Student Volunteer
Nick Couchell (Student Practicum)
Seong Lee -Student Community Service

Appendix One

Health Education in a Free Medical Clinic During Covid19 Epidemic, Spring 2021
By Dave Brangan, MS, CHES, CEO Health Education Consultants, Inc

With the onset of the Covid19 epidemic in 2019, health education in the SC Free Clinics shifted from chronic disease prevention and education to Covid19 prevention and education. New responsibilities at the Newberry Free Medical Clinic included screening patients before entry into the clinic area for symptoms of Covid19, if they traveled to and returned from a country with high numbers of Covid19 cases, and if they (the patients) had been around anyone with Covid19 including family members and friends. All patients had their temperatures taken before entering the clinic area. Patients were given locations for Covid19 testing and vaccine sites. Some of the patients were given appointments for the vaccine via laptop computer and the VAM system.

Patients testing positive to Covid19 were given nutrition education to boost their immune system. Using the latest research online, three-day meal plans were developed with an emphasis on high protein foods, fruits, and vegetables. Patients with Covid19 and those "at risk" were given additional education and counseling regarding social distancing, hand washing, and other precautionary measures to stop the spread of the virus including proper face protection and ways the virus can be transmitted such as airborne transmission or touching others. Finally, Health Education Consultants Inc published weekly updates on their Facebook page which included the number of new infections, number of tests completed, deaths, ICU bed utilization and percent positive from testing. Additional advice was given on the Facebook page regarding social distancing, covering the mouth when sneezing and the proper use of the protective mask.

All patients entering the Free Medical Clinics served by Health Education Consultants received Covid19 education, practiced social distancing, had faced protection, and were educated regarding signs and symptoms of Covid19 infection. In addition, all patients were encouraged to get tested and receive one of the vaccines (Pfizer, Johnson and Johnson or Moderna) when they became available. In general, almost all patients going in public places in the Newberry area such as Walmart and other shopping areas practiced social distancing and had face protection. In the clinic areas, strict rules regarding social distancing and face protection are still in place as of July 2021. All patients were encouraged to get the vaccine.

The Health Educator has direct contact and communication with the patients attending clinic which puts the health educator in a unique and valuable position. The health educator can assess and deliver patient education tailored to the degree of understanding, cultural background, and literacy level. Patients were given one-page hand-outs with Covid19 signs and symptoms, prevention, and testing information. All educational handouts were from the Centers for Disease Control or the South Carolina Department of Health. In a way, the health educator was a key person within the clinic area for Covid19 prevention and education.

The challenge for the health educators was this: how to provide chronic disease prevention and education **and** Covid19 prevention simultaneously. Those "at risk" for Covid19 were older patients with diabetes, hypertension, heart disease and obesity which is roughly 80 percent of the patient population attending the SC Free Medical Clinics! Health Education

Consultants was blessed to have three USC pre-med students: Megan Jones, Allison Ernest and Nicolas Cutshall who were doing their Exercise Science practicum with Health Education Consultants, Inc. in the Spring of 2021. Little did they know when they signed up for their practicum that they would be working on the front lines of the Covid19 epidemic!

In summary, the Covid19 epidemic has demonstrated the need and efficacy of public health education and clinic-based patient education as well. Individual patient education and community health education have played an important role in the reduction of new Covid19 cases reported to the South Carolina Department of Health.

We appreciate everyone's support as we work through the epidemic.

Dave Brangan, MS, CHES
CEO, Health Education Consultants, Inc
Healthedconsults@aol.com

Appendix Two

Testimonies – Health Education Consultants, Inc

From: Newberry Free Medical Clinic, Newberry, South Carolina

December 12, 2019

Greta Tolan

My name is Greta Toland and I have diabetes, congestive heart failure, and high blood pressure. Two years ago, my body was swollen due to retaining fluids. I didn't have a doctor, so I went to the Newberry Free Medical Clinic where they have been taking good care of me. I also took diabetes classes over at the Newberry Hospital which helped me a lot. They put me on an 1800 calorie diet and my weight went from 329 pounds to 267 pounds. I intend to lose another 50 pounds. I don't do too much walking because of my arthritis so I must really concentrate on my nutrition. I have breathing problems and use medication so that limits my exercise too. I pray and keep going. I take my medications every day. I drink a lot of water. The Newberry Free Medical Clinic has helped me a whole lot. Everyone at the Newberry Free Medical Clinic is the best! They treat me nicely. I don't know what I would do without them!

December 5, 2019

Frances Dunbar

My name is Frances Dunbar and I have been attending the Newberry Free Medical Clinic for about two years now. I attended the diabetes classes at the Newberry Hospital and talked with Mr. Dave about controlling my diabetes through nutrition and exercise. I weighed 220 pounds at the time and now I weigh 134 pounds, came off the insulin and just take two tablets a day for my diabetes. I feel great. Also, my father inspired me by losing a lot of weight and got off his medications.

The first thing I did was back off the dinner table. I quit fried and spicy foods. I followed the meal plan and menus given to me by Mr. Dave. I cut way back on starches and eat more vegetables and fruit. I walk every day for about a mile. I try and walk fast. I pray to God to keep me healthy as I have eight grandkids to take care of ranging from age 2 to age 14. I thank the Newberry Free Medical Clinic for all the help that they have given to me.

October 21, 2019

Brenda Swittenburg

Hi, I am Brenda Swittenburg and I have been smoking cigarettes since age 21 and I am 49 years old now. I smoked one to two packs of cigarettes a day. While at work, I had to go outside or the lady's room. I wanted to quit and didn't know how. I was in the hospital for pneumonia and had trouble breathing. They were testing my lungs for breathing problems. The doctor said I should quit smoking and I did! It has been one month now, and I have quit for good. I made up my mind to do it and there is no going back. I have more energy, look better and have saved a lot of money. I just wish everyone would quit smoking.

October 17, 2019

Mary Glass

My name is Mary Glass, and I am 60 years old. I have been going to the Newberry Free Medical Clinic for about 10 years and have had nothing but great service from everyone that worked with me. My doctors have been top notch in ordering good directions for a healthy life. When I first came to the clinic, it was determined I was diabetic, and I weighed 185-200 pounds for a long time.

About a year ago, I received advice on my eating habits, exercising and other good habits to practice every day. Because of this, within a year's time, I have gotten my weight down to 130 as of today. My blood sugar stays around 106. I am very pleased and happy due to all the good advice and help from my doctor and staff from the Newberry Free Medical Clinic. Thank you so much!

September 19, 2019

Florence Anderson

My name is Florence Anderson and I started coming to the Newberry Free Medical Clinic in April of 2019. I weighed 220 pounds at the time. I have diabetes and I thought I better do something about this weight. I went to see Mr. Dave and we talked about food to eat and food to avoid. I realized I was eating a lot of starches like bread, potatoes, lasagna, and bread rolls. I wasn't walking or exercising at the time and now I cut the grass and might even walk too much. I walk in the neighborhood. I walk fast for the first part and then slow on the way back. I walk every other day. My weight is 196 today and I plan to lose more. I feel great. My advice to someone who wants to lose weight is to make up your mind and go for it! And stick to it. Avoid the starches!

August 6, 2019

Kathy Cromer

Hi. I am Kathy Cromer, and I am a patient at the Newberry Free Medical Clinic. I was always feeling tired, so I started going to the doctor to find out why I was always feeling tired so much. I asked my doctor if I had high blood pressure and was I a diabetic? He said I had some of the symptoms of diabetes. But before I got a chance to find out, I was going partially blind for a while. They put me in the hospital for seven days. My blood sugar was 697 at the time. But since I have been doing my diet right, plus exercise, eating the right foods, I feel better. I have lost about 15 pounds. When I started my health education plan, I weighed 249 and now I weigh 220 pounds, but my goal is 185 pounds, and I am going to reach my goal. So, you can do it if you want to. Diabetes is nothing to play around with. Your life is more important!

June 19, 2019

Latonya Plummer

My name is LaTonya P. Plummer. I am a patient at the Free Clinic of Newberry. I was diagnosed as diabetic two years ago. I am no longer a diabetic because I have lost 15 pounds since being diagnosed. Everyone needs to realize that weight plays a major part with a lot of health issues. If you are not sure of how much weight you should loose, just ask your doctor and he or she will let you know. Another thing, if you are a smoker, that is not good for your health either. I have quit smoking and am very proud of myself. You can quit also; it just takes a lot of willpower and a lot of prayers. Dr. Bradbury and Dr. Thompson helped me along the way. LaTonya P. Plummer.

March 20, 2019

Beverly Hawkins

My name is Beverly Hawkins and six months ago I came to the Newberry Free Medical Clinic and was told that I was a borderline diabetic by the doctor. My weight was 280 pounds and the doctor said if I lost weight, I could keep from becoming a diabetic. I talked with Mr. Dave, and he explained the diet sheets and how to lose weight. I changed a lot of my eating habits. I don't eat fried foods anymore; I broil and bake. I use an air cooker without cooking oils and cut back on meats. I cut way back on Pepsi soda drinks; I make unsweetened tea and just add a spoon full of sugar like Mr. Dave said. I love my fruits and vegetables, collard greens, dry beans, and dark green lettuce. I cut back on my portion size, and I don't feel as full anymore. Changing my eating habits was a decision I had to make, and I am sticking with it. I weigh 256 pounds now, down from 280 and I intend to lose more. I even bought a new scale. I exercise by doing chair exercise and walking in the yard. And now my daughter is losing weight. I guess I am an inspiration to her! I thank the Newberry Free Clinic for keeping me healthy and keeping me from becoming a person with diabetes!

March 5, 2019

Helen Stein

My name is Helen Stein and I have been attending the Newberry Free Medical Clinic for about 5 years now. My weight used to be 235 pounds and now I am down to 214. I still have a way to go to lose more weight, but I am getting there. I have talked to the patient educator and staff at the clinic about ways to control my blood pressure and improve my nutrition. I have cut out most of the starches and sweets, drink unsweetened tea and drink more water. I don't use any salt. I am exercising the best I can with a bad knee (some arthritis), and I work part time in a convenience store. I like to keep busy. My blood pressure is good, and I have no stress. I take just one low dose blood pressure pill. I feel healthy and appreciate all the help from the Newberry Free Clinic for all they have done for me.

29 January 2019

Brenda Werts

My name is Brenda Werts and I have been coming to the Newberry Free Clinic for several years. I have learned a lot about healthy eating, cutting back on salt, and exercising to control my blood pressure. I use sea salt now and walk two miles a day in my neighborhood to keep my heart pumping. I take my medications faithfully everyday with my breakfast. I have cut my smoking from a pack a day to just 2-3 cigarettes per day and I know I will quit eventually. My weight is within normal range, and I feel a whole lot better. No stress, no headaches and I am good to go! I will be getting my Medicare card in a few months, and I appreciate the help from the people at the Newberry Free Medical Clinic.

December 19, 2018

Dorothy Jackson

My name is Dorothy Jackson and I have been a patient at the Newberry Free Medical Clinic for three years now. I am 55 years old. My great grandmother had diabetes and required several amputations, and I did not want that to happen to me. I weighed 186 pounds at the time. I decided to learn all I could about diabetes prevention and education. I read a lot of books about diabetes, attended health classes through the Oak Grove Presbyterian church I talked with Mr. Dave about the right food choices and serving sizes of fruits, vegetables, starches, and meats to control my blood sugar. I wanted to prevent the onset of symptoms of full-blown diabetes. My eyes were already getting blurry. My weight from 186 to 153 pounds. I work as a custodian, so I am exercising all day, plus I am a fast walker! I do not eat sweets anymore, I avoid them. I read labels and look for low calorie foods, especially sodas. I drink water now. My A1c has dropped to under 6.2 and that is considered good. The Newberry Free Medical Clinic has helped me a lot through their support, advice, and medical treatment. I learned from my grandmother too.

September 20, 2018

Charles Marshall

This is my testimony. I was working full time as a machine operator for 21 years and was laid off 3 years ago. Then I lost my health insurance. I had diabetes at the time and had nowhere to go to see a doctor. I was skipping my medications and getting depressed. I didn't have a prescription to get my Metformin. Dr. Cory Hunt referred me to the Newberry Free Clinic. My diabetes was getting worse, and my blood sugar was high when I came to the clinic. Then things began to improve. You might say God sent me to the clinic He wasn't through with me yet. I learned what foods to eat and not eat, did some exercise, and now have some exercise equipment at home which helps me control my diabetes. I am very thankful for the Newberry Free Clinic for helping me stay healthy and the support they have given me. Every chance I get, I stop by and say thank you. I thank God for the Free Clinic.

June 5, 2018

Patricia Dale

My name is Patricia Dale and I have been attending the Newberry Free Medical Clinic for 4 years now. When I first started coming to the clinic, I had diabetes and was overweight. I had a difficult time controlling my blood sugar because I really didn't eat the right foods and didn't exercise. I have a stationary bike at home but never used it. I finally decided to do something because my blood sugar was getting very difficult to control. I received patient education about what foods to eat and kept the papers in my kitchen and started the meal for 1600 calories. I cut back on my carbohydrates, especially pasta, white bread, and fruit juice. Now I eat fresh fruit and vegetables. I eat boiled eggs for breakfast, roast my vegetables and use olive oil. I also plan my meals. For exercise, I do a lot of yard work and now use my stationary bike and have lost over 50 pounds. I have been working with my doctor to cut back on my diabetic medications. With diabetes, you must be determined to make some changes and make the right choices. I feel much better now and really appreciate the services of the Newberry Free Medical Clinic.

May 31, 2018
Carol Williams

My name is Carol Williams and I have been coming to the Newberry Free Medical Clinic for 4 years. I was taking blood pressure medicine which I didn't like but had to do it. I decided I wanted to come off the medication, so I followed the meal plan given to me by the patient educator and lost 15 pounds. I also started walking about a mile each day for 30 to 60 minutes in the neighborhood which made me feel healthier. I started managing stress which I think contributed to the high blood pressure. Well, the daily exercise took care of that. I don't smoke. My goal is to weigh around 172 pounds. The Clinic has really helped me get healthy. I have been able to quite my blood pressure medicine! I am thankful for all the services provided to me by the Newberry Free Medical Clinic. I thank God for putting me in the right place at the right time.

November 1, 2018
Kavonne Ruff

My name is Kavonne Ruff, and I have been coming to the Newberry Free Clinic for four years. At the time my diabetes blood sugar was not under control. The doctors started me on diabetes medication and that worked for a while. Then I started a diabetes nutrition plan and my blood sugar started going down. I have cut out noodles, rice, pasta, sweets, and all fried foods. I eat everything in moderation. I Love eating salads and whole wheat breads. I drink a lot more water now and I didn't used to do that. Also, I drink the low-calorie green tea (citrus) which I love. My A1c is 7 today which is down from 13 at the end of March 2017. Dr. Thompson took me off metformin and now I take just one Glipizide pill a day for my diabetes. I really didn't know anything about diabetes, and it was scary. It was very helpful to talk with the patient educator about the meal plans, reading the pamphlets and booklets. I am appreciative of the services at the Newberry Free Clinic.

October 10, 2017
Timothy Thompson

This is Timothy Thompson. I have quit smoking for 4 months now. I have been smoking since age 14. I thought it was cool, but it's not. I have had problems with my blood pressure so I thought this would be a good time to quit, so I have been slacking off my daily cigarettes. Whenever I get the urge to smoke, I drink water or have a Lifesaver candy. Butterscotch is my favorite flavor and seems to work for me. I have more energy now and seem less agitated. If I can get past the mornings, I am OK. I am learning to drink coffee without a cigarette. Since I quit smoking, my blood pressure is better controlled. I have cut back on salt and am taking my blood pressure at home with a blood pressure monitoring machine. I thank the Newberry Free Medical Clinic for helping me get healthy so I can enjoy my life!

September 26, 2917

Ann Stein

I have lost 20 pounds since the beginning of this year. I have been coming to the clinic and talking with the patient educator on how to lose weight. I stay away from starches like bread and rice. I cut back on mayonnaise and sweets as well. All I drink is water and unsweetened tea. I quit drinking Mountain Dew also. I do a lot of exercise, mostly walking at least four times a week. I don't eat meat like I used to and eat more vegetables than anything. I sleep much better at night. The meal plans given to me by Mr. Dave have been very helpful. My blood pressure has dropped as well.

June 8, 2017

Nadean Johnson

I have been smoking cigarettes for most of my life and at age 57, I have decided to quit. I have two grandchildren, a boy and a girl, and I would like to see them grow up. I hated being around smokers, but I just went along with the crowd for most of my life. A lot of times, I smoked because I was bored. And I was just throwing money away. I have been attending the Newberry Free Clinic for several years. They have been very supportive and encouraged me to quit. I have been quit for three months now. I drink a lot of water, chew gum, and exercise. My blood pressure is controlled, and my goal is to lose weight and stop taking medicine. I have more energy and food tastes better. I feel as though I have quit for good.

May 18, 2017

Clinton Huff

I have been a patient at the Newberry Free Medical Clinic since 2008. I had a prostate exam at the clinic, and it turned out to be cancer of the prostate. I began treatment right away with chemotherapy shots and some radiation. I am happy to say that I am in complete remission, thanks to the Lord and the staff at the Newberry Free Medical clinic. I think all men aged 40 and over should have regular prostate exams and take care of themselves. I would recommend anyone without health insurance to go to the Free Clinic. The staff members are very caring and treat you like a person. Talking with Mr. Dave, the patient educator, has really helped my health and well-being also. I have Medicare now and I thank the Lord for all the services I have received from the Newberry Free Medical Clinic.

April 11, 2017

Margie Sleigh

I have been smoking for 41 years since I was age 14. I have quit smoking for 61 days now and it has been one of the best decisions I have made in my life. I have more energy now and my sense of smell is coming back. Food tastes better! Quitting smoking is a mind thing. You must make the decision to quit and then stick to it. It is a commitment. To help me get through the urge to smoke, I drink water and sometimes chew sugarless Lifesavers. I thank the Newberry Free Medical Clinic for their encouragement and support!

January 19, 2017

Wildrick Cook

My name is Wildrick Cook and I am a patient at the Newberry Free Medical clinic. I am 44 years old. Last July of 2016, I had a stroke. I weighed 260 pounds. I had high blood pressure and diabetes. My doctor said I was going to have a stroke, but I didn't listen to him. I ignored the fact that I had high blood pressure. I woke up one morning last July and had trouble getting out of bed. I couldn't move my right side. That afternoon I went to the Emergency Room at Newberry hospital, and they admitted me right away. They didn't do any surgery but ran a lot of heart tests. I was referred to physical therapy and sent to patient education classes at the hospital where I learned about what foods to eat and what foods not to eat. I have cut back on salt and greasy foods and now weigh 216 pounds. The staff at the Newberry Hospital has been great and am expected to make a full recovery. I am also reading Mr. Dave's Diabetes Health Education Workbook which has been very helpful also. I thank the Free Clinic and Newberry Hospital physical therapy for all their help

December 19, 2016

Carl Williams

My name is Carl Williams and I have been coming to the Newberry Free Medical Clinic for about three years. My blood pressure was high at the time, but the Free Medical Clinic gave me medication to control it. Since then, I have come off medication by losing weight, cutting back on salt and managing stress. I plan to stay off medication if I can by exercising and trying to eat the right kinds of foods. I am very appreciative of the services provided by the Newberry Free Medical Clinic.

November 14, 2016
Candice Johnson

My name is Candice Johnson, and I began coming to the Newberry Free Clinic approximately one year ago. At the time, my blood pressure was extremely high, and my overall health was at stake. Thanks to the kindness and professional help of the staff at the Free Clinic I am happy to report that one year later, my blood pressure is under control. The clinic has helped me not only through medication but a change in lifestyle habits. I now exercise more, eat less salt, and have my smoking habit reduced to a minimum with full confidence I can soon quit. I am greatly appreciative of the services offered by those at the Newberry Free Medical Clinic.

July 5, 2016
Tammy Harrison

My name is Tammy Harrison. I visited the Newberry Free Clinic in May 2016 with my blood sugar for diabetes being extremely high. I had visited the Emergency Room twice in one week, earlier that month with my blood sugar being 500-600. After two long waits at the ER, I promised myself that this wasn't going to happen again. I vowed to eat right, cutting down on helpings, cutting out foods that I didn't need to eat, exercising regularly and putting myself first instead of others.
    During the visit to the Free Clinic, I received health education about diabetes and how to control it. Being a nursing student at Piedmont Technical College, I already knew a lot about this disease. Since visiting the clinic, the last time, my blood sugar is much better, usually between 100 – 170. I have lost almost 10 pounds and I feel 100 percent better. I feel like a new person. I still have some weight to lose but with determination, the help of the Free Clinic and Jesus, I will get it done!!

Kristy Wells

DOB: 4 January 60

August 12, 2021

My name is Kristy Wells and I have been working steadily, however with no health insurance. I started coming to the Newberry Free Medial Clinic about two years. The clinic has helped me with my health, all the tests I need to stay healthy, including blood tests, and mammograms. I have used the WelVista program at the Newberry Free Medical Clinic which has helped me get my medications. Dr. Bradbury has been wonderful providing medical care. If the Newberry Free Medical Clinic was not here, I would probably die because I have no other place to go. The staff is very professional and friendly. The services are prompt with little or no waiting. I am very thankful for the services here at the clinic.

Shirley Brown

DOB: Nov 11, 1959

August 12, 2021

I have been going to the Newberry Free Clinic for about 5 years now. I didn't have any health insurance and I was not working. I have diabetes and my blood sugar was "wild and out of control." I didn't have any money for medications. I was referred to the Free Clinic by Dr. Lovelace. My health started improving right away. Everyone at the clinic was helpful and had the most beautiful personalities and I love them! Thank God for the Clinic! Let's keep that clinic moving and grooving. I have always been treated with the ultimate respect and I love coming to the clinic. j

Judy Watts

DOB: 11-2661

August 12, 2021

I have been coming to the Newberry Free Clinic since 2015. I didn't have any insurance and I had medical problems like high blood pressure and some other problems. I started receiving my medications through the clinic. My blood pressure is now under control and so is my thyroid. The staff was great, and everyone is nice. The clinic also has helped me with doctors who are specialists including mental health and GYN. The patient educator has also helped with my diet and exercise. I do not know what I would do without the Free Medical clinic, and I am thankful for their services.

Leanne Patterson

June 20,1966

August 12, 2021

I have been going to the Newberry Free Medical clinic for about 5 years now. I had my own doctor but couldn't keep up the payments. I was not working at the time. I had medical problems which needed attention right away. Dr. Thompson is a very good doctor and has been very helpful. I get my medications from the Free Clinic also to help with the pain in my knee. I do not know where I would go if it were not for the Free Clinic. I would recommend the services at the Free Clinic. They are "right on." They make sure I get my medications. The staff are good listeners, honest and I appreciate them. The staff does not beat around the bush and if there is something wrong, they will tell me. I am thankful for their services.

Jean Brown

DOB: 3 Jul 66

August 12, 2021

I have been going to the Free Clinic for about a year now. I had no insurance and I had diabetes and it was not completely under control. I could not afford to pay a family doctor. Everyone at the clinic has been very helpful. I couldn't afford my medicine. I had lots of questions and received lots of good health information. My blood sugar was high, and I got it under control by diet and exercise. Dr. Bradbury was very helpful, as were the rest of the staff at the clinic. I am grateful for all the services at the clinic and would recommend the clinic to my friends. A big thank you to everyone.

Appendix Three

State of South Carolina
Office of the Secretary of State

The Honorable Mark Hammond

5/22/2023

Health Education Consultants, Inc.
Dave Brangan
PO BOX 308 IRMO,
SC29063-0308

RE: Exemption Confirmation Charity Public ID: P35027

Dear Dave Brangan:

This letter confirms that the Secretary of State's Office has received and accepted your Application for Exemption. **If you submitted your Application for Exemption using the Charities Online Filing System, this letter of confirmation has been issued pending further review by Division of Public Charities staff.**

The exemption for your charitable organization will expire on 5/15/2023. If any of the information on your Application for Exemption form changes throughout the course of the year, please contact our office to make updates. It is important that this information remain updated so that our office can keep you informed of any changes that may affect your charitable organization. Additionally, if at any time your charitable organization no longer qualifies for an exemption, the organization must immediately register with the Secretary of State's Office. Please note that failure to comply with the registration provisions of the Solicitation of Charitable Funds Act may result in fines of up to $2,000.00 for each separate violation.

If you have any questions or concerns, please visit our website at www.sos.sc.gov or contact our office using the contact information below.

Sincerely,

Kimberly S. Wickersham
Director, Division of Public Charities

INTERNAL REVENUE SERVICE
P. O. BOX 2508
CINCINNATI, OH 45201

DEPARTMENT OF THE TREASURY

Date: **NOV 06 2014**

HEALTH EDUCATION CONSULTANTS INC
PO BOX 308
IRMO, SC 29063-0000

Employer Identification Number:
20-1025989
DLN:
26053648001234
Contact Person:
MARIA S TRITCH   ID# 31549
Contact Telephone Number:
(513) 263-4453
Accounting Period Ending:
December 31
Public Charity Status:
509(a)(2)
Form 990/990-EZ/990-N Required:
Yes
Effective Date of Exemption:
September 2, 2014
Contribution Deductibility:
Yes
Addendum Applies:
Yes

Dear Applicant:

We're pleased to tell you we determined you're exempt from federal income tax under Internal Revenue Code (IRC) Section 501(c)(3). Donors can deduct contributions they make to you under IRC Section 170. You're also qualified to receive tax deductible bequests, devises, transfers or gifts under Section 2055, 2106, or 2522. This letter could help resolve questions on your exempt status. Please keep it for your records.

Organizations exempt under IRC Section 501(c)(3) are further classified as either public charities or private foundations. We determined you're a public charity under the IRC Section listed at the top of this letter.

Based on the information you submitted on your application, we approved your request for reinstatement under Section 7 of Revenue Procedure 2014-11. Your effective date of exemption, as listed at the top of this letter, is the submission date of your application.

If we indicated at the top of this letter that you're required to file Form 990/990-EZ/990-N, our records show you're required to file an annual information return (Form 990 or Form 990-EZ) or electronic notice (Form 990-N, the e-Postcard). If you don't file a required return or notice for three consecutive years, your exempt status will be automatically revoked.

If we indicated at the top of this letter that an addendum applies, the enclosed addendum is an integral part of this letter.

For important information about your responsibilities as a tax-exempt organization, go to www.irs.gov/charities. Enter "4221-PC" in the search bar

Letter 5436

HEALTH EDUCATION CONSULTANTS INC

to view Publication 4221-PC, Compliance Guide for 501(c)(3) Public Charities, which describes your recordkeeping, reporting, and disclosure requirements.

Sincerely,

Tamera Ripperda

Director, Exempt Organizations

Appendix Four —

Healthcare Reform Articles from the Orangeburg Newspaper "The Times and Democrat" written in 2010 and 2011 (still applies today).

July 27, 2010

Health and Wellness – Part One

Health and wellness are two concepts we will be hearing more about as the health care reform law moves forward. When health and wellness are discussed, the discussion usually turns to nutrition and exercise - subjects most Americans would rather not talk about. We are well-accustomed to our fast-food drive-thru, fancy restaurants, convenience stores and microwave ovens. And we have our 32-inch wide-screen digital televisions, laptop computers complete with Internet connections, PlayStations and Xboxes, DVDs and VCRs, video games, and portable MP3 and iPods that will play movies.

What is wrong with this picture? Some would say nothing. However, an observation of the people who make repeat trips to the salad bar would reveal the obvious - most Americans are either overweight or obese! And being overweight or obese is laying the groundwork for diabetes, hypertension, heart disease and all the complications that accompany these chronic diseases.

Nutrition is still as simple as following the food pyramid - eating your fruits and vegetables, meats, starches, and fats in moderation throughout the day. And losing weight is quite simple: You must burn off more calories than you take in. If someone is eating 2,000 calories per day and burning 1,000 calories, then the remaining 1,000 calories are stored as fat. There must be a balance between food consumed and food burned through daily activities and exercise. There is no need to run out and purchase a commercial diet plan.

As a professional educator, we do not use the word "diet" because of its negative connotations - we call it "meal planning." Considering a person's daily activities, a meal plan is written using the major food groups approved by the American Dietetic Association and the American Diabetes Association. If a person sits around and watches television all day, then that person would need approximately 1,200 calories. If they work construction or another physically demanding job, then they would need 2,200 calories. Most people need between 1,600 and 1,800 calories.

I asked one of my patients who came into the clinic if they exercised. Their response? "Well, I walk to the mailbox and back." While this is a step in the right direction, the walking must be brisk to burn calories. It should be for at least 20 or 30 minutes to be beneficial. Any exercise that is continuous and aerobic (getting the heart beating faster) would count, including yard work, biking, tennis, mowing the lawn and housework. Individuals should commit to a regular exercise program at a regular time and place.

Nutrition and exercise go hand in hand. You really cannot have one without the other. If you have a meal plan without exercise, it will be much more difficult, and vice versa. It does take commitment for weight management to be successful, and it is hard work. However, like anything else, it becomes easier with time and practice. In the long run, it will be worth it, as your body reaches a natural weight for your height and body build. Your metabolism will see to that.

Weight loss is not about the numbers - it is about a lifestyle change. When talking about health and wellness, we are really talking about a lifestyle change, with nutrition and exercise forming the foundation to prevent chronic diseases. There is no time like the present to start!

*Dave Brangan is a member of the South Carolina Association for the Advancement of Health Education and a health educator at the Orangeburg-Calhoun Free Medical Clinic. He can be reached by e-mail at **DaveB72@aol.com**.*

June 15, 2010

Employer Based Health Insurance

One of the more complex provisions of the Patient Protection and Affordable Care Act passed on March 23 is how employers will provide health care to employees. To fully understand all the provisions, one must spend considerable time reading and re-reading the law, and then there are the exceptions to the law which must be considered.

For starters, by Jan. 1, 2014, all employers with 200 or more employees must automatically enroll their employees into a health insurance plan offered by the employer. The employee may opt out of coverage if he or she already has insurance. For employers with less than 200 employees, there are exceptions and other options that are quite detailed. For now, I will describe the general concepts that guide the details.

The term we hear most frequently is employer tax credit. Tax credits have been around for years as a way for the government to provide incentives to increase productivity and in jobs programs to get people employed. In the health care reform law, the tax credit is for businesses with 50 employees or less that are enrolling their employees into a medical insurance program. The tax credit can be up to 32 percent of the cost of the insurance plan per employee. This provision of the law is supposed to start as early as 2011, and the Internal Revenue Service already has its website up-to-date and ready to answer frequently asked questions.

For employers with 50 or more employees, apparently there are no tax credits. Instead, if the employer does not offer a health care insurance plan, that company can be fined up to $2,000 per full-time employee. This provision does not take effect until Jan. 1, 2014. However, there are options for employers. Do you remember the state-run health exchanges from the previous articles? Employers will have the option to assist their employees to enroll in the exchanges. The employer may offer their own medical insurance plan, or the employer may give the employee a voucher to enroll in the state-run health insurance exchanges. However, the caveat here is that the dollar amount of the voucher is only equal to the employer's portion of the insurance cost. This is usually almost 32 percent of the premium. The employee may be going to the health insurance exchange with a voucher to pay part of the premium, and the employee would have to pay the balance. The bottom line is that every employee will have medical insurance regardless of the size of the company. There does not appear to be any provisions for the temporary or seasonal worker.

There may be a few foreseeable problems here with these provisions. It looks like a good deal for small businesses. However, for the rest of the businesses in our economy, there are no tax credits. Employers may very well pass the rising cost of medical insurance to the employee. In other words, the employer will pay less, and the employee will pay more, or he or she may be off to the state-run health insurance exchanges.

Like many of the other provisions of the law, we will have to adopt a wait-and-see approach to whether this health care reform law will work. As many of the authors of the law have stated, it is not perfect and not meant to be perfect. One might say it is "a work in progress." At least the wheels of the Patient Protection and Affordable Care Act are going forward.

*Dave Brangan is a member of the South Carolina Association for the Advancement of Health Education and a health educator at the Orangeburg-Calhoun Free Medical Clinic. He can be reached by e-mail at **DaveB72@aol.com**.*

June 1, 2010

Healthcare and Preexisting Conditions

When discussing health care and pre-existing conditions, there is no shortage of stories from Americans who have had a major or minor health problem and were denied medical insurance due to a "pre-existing condition."

When my wife and I arrived in South Carolina in August 1988, and I began employment as a public health educator with the South Carolina Department of Health in Orangeburg. I immediately enrolled in a group health insurance with my employer. My wife and I had been married only a few months, and to our joy, we received the news that she was pregnant with our first child. We found an OB-GYN doctor in September 1988, and the due date was May 26, 1989. To make a long story short, when the physician's office sent in the first claim for an office visit, it was denied due to a pre-existing condition! The insurance company said that my wife was pregnant - that is, conception occurred - prior to arriving in the state and prior to my employment and group insurance; therefore, it was a pre-existing condition! It took several phone calls from my supervisor, who happened to be a physician, and that decision was reversed.

One of the priorities of President Barack Obama's health care reform is the elimination of pre-existing conditions. The above story is almost facetious; however, there are many stories about pre-existing conditions that are much more serious. Section 101 of the health care reform law addressed this problem immediately - or at least within 90 days of enactment of the law - by establishing a temporary national high-risk pool program. This section of the law is designed specifically for people who were denied insurance coverage due to a pre-existing health condition or have been dropped from their insurance coverage due to catastrophic illness. In other words, these are folks who are "uninsurable."

The key words here are "temporary" and "high-risk pool program." Let us take a closer look at these two key words.

"Temporary" means just that. People who are uninsurable are placed in a temporary insurance program until the health exchanges can be organized and become operational. This will take at least three or four years. Some states already have high-risk pools established by state legislatures, including South Carolina.

The guidelines for entry in South Carolina's high-risk pool are like the health care reform guidelines - having a medical condition, not being able to find insurance coverage, and living at or near the federal poverty level financially. It should be noted that one must still pay a premium or monthly fee, though at a reduced rate. The high-risk insurance pool is operated by the state's Department of Insurance.

The other key word is "high-risk pool." The question is, will it really work? As of December 2008, S.C.'s high-risk pool had 2,328 enrolled members. Today, that number could easily double if the funds were available. Eventually, the federal and state governments must come together and figure out a way to fund this program and provide effective health care insurance, at least on a temporary basis. According to the Kaiser Foundation, which organizes and publishes information about health care reform on their website, at least $5 billion is set aside for the high-risk pools. Hopefully, this will be enough money to supplement existing high-risk pools in some 33 states and help start new pools in states with no programs.

By 2014, the health care exchanges will be up and running, and the people in the high-risk pools will transition to the exchange. This will be the topic for my next column as the health care reform journey continues. Feel free to e-mail me with comments or questions.

*Dave Brangan is a member of the South Carolina Association for the Advancement of Health Education and a health educator at the Orangeburg-Calhoun Free Medical Clinic. He can be reached by e-mail at **DaveB72@aol.com**.*

August 24, 2010

Healthcare Reform Progress

It has been five months since the Patient Care and Affordability Act, also known as health care reform, became law in the United States. So far, public opinion polls are split - approximately 50 percent of Americans have a favorable view of the law, and the remaining 50 percent have an unfavorable view of it. This might be a suitable time for a progress report regarding the law and to perhaps address some of the concerns and controversies.

In just five months, there has been quite a bit of progress. Here is the short list:

1. Children 26 years of age and younger can remain on their parents' insurance plans.

2. For seniors on Medicare, work has begun to close the doughnut hole: the amount seniors must pay for their medications - and qualifying seniors have received checks for $250.

3. Patients who have been denied insurance due to preexisting conditions have been directed to their state's insurance pool for assistance.

4. A temporary insurance pool has been established for employers who have provide health insurance for retired employees between 55 and 64 years of age who are ineligible for Medicare.

5. Tax credits are available for employers with 25 employees or less and who earn $50,000 or less.

6. Insurance companies are prohibited from putting lifetime limits on the dollar amount of coverage.

While I am not an expert on health insurance, this is an impressive start. We still have a long way to go, especially with Medicaid, but a journey of a thousand miles begins with the first step. And remember, it is not always about the money, in terms of how we will pay for it, but the allocation or reallocation of money for Medicaid and coverage for the uninsured.

There are some 13 states whose attorney generals are going to challenge the constitutionality of the Patient Care and Affordability Act. I have not seen the specifics of the challenge. However, it refers to the requirement for individuals to pay for their health care insurance. We will have to wait and see how this plays out in the legal system. In the meantime, most of us who have insurance are already paying for it. Even seniors on Medicare must pay monthly for their insurance, which they thought was going to be free. People living at or below the poverty level are exempt from purchasing their own health insurance. And there are an endless list of exceptions and circumstances for everyone. But the rationale for the required health care purchase is that the young people, who normally do not get sick, will be helping the older people by adding to the pool of money to help pay the cost of doctors' fees and hospitalization for the older folks. Some people say this is not fair but remember the younger folks will be older folks someday.

No one likes to be required to pay anything, though we do anyway. We pay for our driver's license, pay property taxes to get our plates renewed each year, pay federal and state taxes, sanitation taxes, social security, gasoline taxes, annual fees at the country club, etc. Therefore, we are already being required to pay for things we don't necessarily want or agree with. I would think health care would be a priority among our required spending.

The Patient Care and Affordability Act has a long way to go and, as stated previously, it is not perfect. It will take the collective will of Congress - Democrats and Republicans - and the American people to get the job done. It will take patience and spending our money wisely.

November 23, 2010

Law and Politics

The midterm elections are over, and the people have spoken! I am not sure what was spoken, although health care reform kept coming up in the debates. To make a long story short, the Republicans gained a majority of seats in the House of Representatives and gained a few seats in the U.S. Senate, though not a majority. What does all of this mean?

The Republicans would like to repeal the Patient Protection and Affordable Healthcare Act of March 2010, better known as the health care reform law. They want to repeal and replace it. But replace with what? Unfortunately, the Republicans still have not offered a better health care law that would cover some 40 million people in the United States. President Barack Obama has the upper hand because the law has already been passed and many of its provisions have already taken effect, such as children being on their parent's insurance policies until age 26, pre-existing conditions cannot be the reason for denial of insurance, an emergency re-insurance pool for people over age 50 but not yet 65, and benefits for seniors on Medicare when buying prescription drugs. Also, many prevention and wellness grants have been announced, and worksite wellness programs are being initiated.

Those of us who were diligent students of government will remember how a bill becomes a law. A bill is introduced in the House of Representatives, which is dominated by Republicans. If the Republicans want to pass a bill in the House that repeals the Patient Protection and Affordable Healthcare Act, they may be able to do it. However, the bill would go next to the U.S. Senate for approval, which is dominated by Democrats. It is doubtful if a health care repeal law would go through the Senate dominated by Democrats and the law would remain the same as it is today. Even if a health care repeal law made it through the Senate, the president could still veto it.

Public opinion polls vary on the new health care law. However, time is on the side of the president. As the health care law provisions are phased in, it will be that much more difficult to repeal. Once someone has received a benefit, i.e., from the pre-existing conditions provision, it will be that much more difficult to reverse. There will be public outcry. If President Obama is elected to another term in 2012, then he will push through the critical year of 2014, when Medicaid is expanded to include millions more uninsured people.

*Dave Brangan is a member of the South Carolina Association for the Advancement of Health Education and a health educator at the Orangeburg-Calhoun Free Medical Clinic. He can be reached by e-mail at **DaveB72@aol.com**.*

September 28, 2010

Paying for Healthcare Reform – Part 2

In my previous article on paying for health care reform, I discussed how health care could be paid for by trimming the AIDS program budget and saving money with a reduction of U.S. military forces overseas, particularly in Iraq and Afghanistan. If this is not enough to pay for the health care reform, the new law will raise taxes on pharmaceutical companies, insurance companies, medical supply devices and tanning salons. The taxes are in annual increments and would raise an additional $64.2 billion through 2018. These figures are well-illustrated in the Kaiser Foundation Reports which is the source of information and statistics for these articles on health care reform. This website is very informative and, most importantly, not biased in any way.

When discussing the costs of health care for the uninsured, there are many variables, and some costs are difficult to predict. For example, who can predict the cost of cancer treatments, radiation, and chemotherapy in the year 2014? Undoubtedly, it will cost more than it does today. Therefore, even more revenue is needed to cover the cost of inflation and the spiraling cost of health care, in general. The tax revenues discussed in the previous paragraph may not be available. And the planned taxes on pharmaceutical companies and insurance companies may not work very well because that cost may be passed on to the consumer. Another source of revenue is the requirement that every person, based on income, purchase health insurance, either through private insurance or through the proposed state exchanges. Failure to purchase health insurance will cost an individual nearly $700 per year in penalties, with increases each year that it is not paid.

There will be other ways to raise revenue that will be discussed in future articles. For now, I would like to introduce the subject of compassion, as it relates to health care reform. Compassion has not been part of the American political scene since Jimmy Carter was president from 1976 to 1979. If I recall correctly, this compassion stemmed from his strong religious beliefs based on his Christian faith. Most, if not all, religious beliefs have a form of compassion or love and respect for other people. If other people are suffering and are in need, then there is an implied duty to help that person. This is true for Christians, Hindus, Muslims, and Jews. It is interesting to note that in public opinion polls, most Americans believe in God. The United States Constitution is based on Christian principles. Why not apply these Christian and other religious beliefs to health care reform?

Compassion and love for one's neighbor should be the basis for reform. One might be surprised how many Christians, Hindus, Muslims, and Jewish people would agree with this need. Yes, we need billions of stimulus money to build roads, bridges, and highways, but we need stimulus money to pay for health care, too. It is time to bring compassion back into politics and health care for the uninsured.

Dave Brangan is a member of the South Carolina Association for the Advancement of Health Education and a health educator at the Orangeburg-Calhoun Free Medical Clinic. He can be reached by e-mail at **DaveB72@aol.com**.

July 27, 2010

Prevention and Wellness

Prevention and wellness are finally getting the recognition they deserve and are now part of the new health care reform law passed in March. The overall strategy is sound, and it involves community-based prevention and wellness services, as well.

Effective immediately is the establishment of a National Prevention, Health Promotion and Public Health Council to coordinate the entire strategy with an initial appropriation of $7 billion and $7 billion for each fiscal year up to 2015. A large part of this strategy is to give grants to state and private health service organizations to support the delivery of evidence-based prevention and wellness programs.

One of the major goals is to reduce chronic diseases, such as diabetes, hypertension and heart disease, and address health disparities, especially in rural and frontier areas. All of this will require time, patience, money and, most importantly, participation by the general population, especially those "at risk" for chronic diseases.

There are two aspects to prevention and wellness. Prevention includes physical screenings like mammograms for breast cancer, colonoscopies for colon cancer, immunizations for children and adults, prostate screenings for men, and health risk assessments to determine risks for the chronic diseases. These screenings are physical or diagnostic in nature, and health plans - including Medicare and Medicaid - are required to pay for these screenings. It does not take much effort - the screening or procedure is done, and the results are sent to your doctor, who calls you in and gives you the results. And that is that.

Wellness involves effort in the form of behavior change. The language of the law uses the term "behavior modification," though professional health educators know that behavior cannot be modified - it must be a <u>voluntary change</u> in behavior. What exactly are we talking about here? As a professional health educator, I can tell you when "dealing" with chronic diseases, the discussion usually leads to nutrition and exercise. And, as a professional health educator, I can tell you these are two subjects most South Carolinians would rather not talk about! For now, I will spare you, the reader, further discussion on nutrition and exercise with the promise of a future article devoted to just these two topics.

Another nice provision of the prevention and wellness section of the law is the encouragement of work site wellness programs. Grants will be offered to employers to establish wellness programs on-site, and incentives would be offered to employees who participate. One incentive might be a reduction in cost of the employee's medical insurance. Work site wellness programs are not new to health professionals; however, what is new is the government's encouragement and support of these programs. Hopefully these programs will proliferate among small businesses and large corporations.

If you are uncertain what is meant by health and wellness, you are not alone. A health-and-wellness program begins with a comprehensive risk assessment. This is usually a long questionnaire, or "appraisal," of one's health. It is like a medical history when visiting your physician for the first time. Your risk factors are determined by age, race, gender, weight, nutritional choices, family history for chronic diseases, tobacco use, seat belt use, frequency of exercise, drug and alcohol use, educational level, where you live and your mental health status. A good health risk assessment can predict what diseases you will experience in your lifetime and how long you might live. It is surprisingly accurate. The good news is these diseases are preventable, or at least can be delayed through prevention, health education and wellness programs. However, it does take effort and voluntary behavior changes. More on this in future articles.

*Dave Brangan is a member of the South Carolina Association for the Advancement of Health Education and a health educator at the Orangeburg-Calhoun Free Medical Clinic. He can be reached by e-mail at **DaveB72@aol.com**.*

November 9, 2010

Reform and Mental Health

One of the most overlooked items of the Patient Protection and Affordable Care Act passed in March is the benefit of mental health coverage for individuals suffering from mild and more serious forms of mental illness.

As anyone who works in the mental health profession will tell you, there is a stigma attached to someone who may be experiencing mental health issues. There is no stigma attached to someone with heart disease or lung failure, but there is for someone who seeks treatment for depression, schizophrenia, or bipolar disorder. The health care reform law will indirectly "normalize" mental health - at least to a point where it can be discussed.

Section 5203 of the health care reform law authorizes $30 million dollars each year from 2010 to 2014 loan repayment programs for providers of mental and behavior health services who are willing to work in rural and medically underserved areas, such as Orangeburg County. Additional money will be available for schools of social work, graduate psychology, and professional child and adolescent mental health. There is also money for training in paraprofessional child and adolescent work, as well. Help is on the way.

With the expansion of Medicaid eligibility in 2014 will come an expansion of services, to include mental health services covered by Medicaid. At the present time, in the state of South Carolina, it is very difficult to get Medicaid. As one patient told me at the Orangeburg-Calhoun Free Medical Clinic, "You have to be sick and almost dying to get Medicaid, and by then, it might be too late." For someone with a mental health disease, it is even more difficult to get Medicaid. As a result, mental health issues go untreated. If long-term depression goes untreated, it can lead to suicide. Other untreated mental illness leads to joblessness, homelessness, crime, domestic violence, and the list goes on. Therefore, Medicaid will help those people presently without health care insurance to get the mental health treatment they need, and not wander the streets getting into trouble and filling up the homeless shelters.

A final positive development with health care reform and mental health is the expansion of medications that will be paid for by Medicaid. Many of these drugs are used by physicians in treatment facilities for bipolar disorders, anxiety attacks, depression, and a host of other mental illnesses.

While the expansion of mental health treatment options will not solve all the mental health problems in our society, it will be a start and will help a population that frequently gets neglected. Indirectly, this will help to reduce the stigma attached to mental health and normalize the disease. My next article will discuss the results of the 2010 mid-term elections and how those results might impact the health care reform law.

*Dave Brangan is a member of the South Carolina Association for the Advancement of Health Education and a health educator at the Orangeburg-Calhoun Free Medical Clinic. He can be reached by e-mail at **DaveB72@aol.com**.*

December 21, 2010

Reform and Choices

Christmas time is upon us, and it is time to give thanks for all our blessings. For those of us with health care insurance, Medicare, or Medicaid, this is a blessing. Some 40 million Americans have none of the aforementioned. But for those of us with private health care insurance, this is a mixed blessing, as premiums are expected to rise in January because employers will be shifting costs to employees and insurance companies are expected to raise their rates in anticipation of the new health care reform laws to be phased in over the next four years. It is easy to be pessimistic during these times, with or without health care insurance. However, I would like to offer some choices for you, the reader, during these difficult times.

We all have choices whether to be healthy. Granted, there are those unfortunate people who may have a terminal or debilitating health problem. But for most Americans, we make choices every day - even several times per day - regarding the food we eat, the beverages we drink and whether to engage in physical activity. This might be a good time for all of us to think about nutritious foods and how much we exercise each day. If you are a smoker, this would be a good time to quit. All of this is related, either directly or indirectly to health care reform.

I recall working for a health care organization in Orangeburg several years ago and considered purchasing medical insurance for my family. The premium was a group rate; therefore, it would be a lot cheaper than purchasing it as an individual. However, the monthly premium was high. When investigating a little further, I learned the rates were based on the overall health of the employees who worked for the health care organization. To make a long story short, there was one employee who was a heavy smoker, had lung disease and was required to carry around an oxygen tank. She required numerous trips to the emergency room and hospitalization while working as long as she could. She continued to smoke even with the oxygen tank. Her multiple trips to the emergency room and hospital visits forced the insurance company to raise the monthly premiums for the rest of the employees! She had a choice to quit smoking, which may have improved her lung condition and led to less frequent trips to the hospital and lower monthly premiums.

We indeed have choices - to eat nutritious foods or high sugar and fatty foods; to engage in physical activity for 30 minutes a day or watch TV; to smoke or not to smoke; to over indulge in food portions or limit serving size; to take control of our health and have a positive attitude or be pessimistic and fatalistic; to wear our seat belt or don't wear our seat belt, and whether to drink alcoholic beverages in moderation. For those individuals who take medication for chronic diseases such as diabetes and hypertension, the choice is whether to take their medications as directed by their physician or skip a dose now and then.

We have a new year coming in 2011, so this would be a good time to get started on a healthy lifestyle and make choices that directly affect our health. Merry Christmas to everyone, and a happy and healthy new year!

*Dave Brangan is a member of the South Carolina Association for the Advancement of Health Education and a health educator at the Orangeburg-Calhoun Free Medical Clinic. He can be reached by e-mail at **DaveB72@aol.com**.*

December 7, 2010

Reform and Legal Issues

As Congress prepares to go into recess for the Christmas holidays, there are State Attorney Generals in some 13 states - including South Carolina - preparing legal cases against the new Patient Protection and Affordable Care Act of March 2010. It will be quite interesting to see how this plays out in the courts and how they will make their case.

Some of the attorney generals will undoubtedly make this states' rights issue. Gov.-elect Nikki Haley has implied that South Carolina will take care of our own uninsured population and does not need health care reform to do so. Medicaid dollars usually are approximately 3 to 1 - that is, three federal dollars for each state dollar. I think South Carolina will need federal help to keep the Medicaid program going. The last time I checked South Carolina's budget, there was a deficit, meaning there is no extra money for health care insurance for uninsured residents of South Carolina (an estimated 20 percent of the state's population).

However, the states' rights issue is a strong one that dates to the Civil War, and books have been written about states' rights vs. federal mandates. In my opinion, there are very few federal mandates. At one time, military service was compulsory or mandated, though today it is voluntary. Obviously, federal taxes are mandated if you want to have strong national defense, and Medicare and Social Security are mandatory. These federal taxes come back to benefit the individual, albeit a little later in life.

The attorneys general will also zero in on technicalities of the health care reform law dealing with interstate commerce, contracts, and insurance companies. These legalities are beyond most people, me included, and we will have to wait and observe these proceedings.

It is understandable that someone should not be "forced" to do something or pay for something that they do not want. I do not want to pay for car insurance. However, car insurance is mandated by the state of South Carolina to include liability insurance for medical care in case someone is injured in another car. And if I want to drive a car in South Carolina, I will have to pay for a license along with the insurance. Therefore, everyone benefits from participation in the driving laws of South Carolina: The state receives the fees for driver's license, tags, and registration; the local county receives the property tax; the insurance company receives their compensation, and there is medical coverage (liability) for the other guy who might be injured in an automobile accident.

By now, you see that I am drawing an analogy here, comparing driving in South Carolina with participating in the health care reform law. If we all participate, then we all benefit. And no one gets left behind or left out in the cold.

*Dave Brangan is a member of the South Carolina Association for the Advancement of Health Education and a health educator at the Orangeburg-Calhoun Free Medical Clinic. He can be reached by e-mail at **DaveB72@aol.com**.*

February 11, 2011

Healthcare Reform Debate Continues

Well, it has been almost a year now since the Healthcare Protection and Affordable Care Act was passed by Congress in March 2010. The new law has been in and out of the news several times during the past few months. Readers of this column should be familiar with the provisions of the law that have taken effect immediately: Children can remain on their parent's insurance until the age of 26, pre-existing conditions cannot be a reason for denial of benefits, grants and tax credits are available for small businesses to develop wellness programs, and financial assistance is available for seniors to help pay for their medications. Also, insurance companies cannot drop someone from their policies due to a serious illness. As good as all of this may sound, the health care reform debate is far from over.

Last month, in the United States House of Representatives, a procedural vote was taken to repeal the law. This was led by the Republican majority, and the vote was in favor of the Republicans who want to "replace and repeal." While this was a symbolic act, it put the country on notice that the fight is far from over. The next step was to send the bill to the Senate, which has a Democratic majority. When the vote was taken in the Senate, the Democrats prevailed and the procedural vote to repeal the act was not passed. The Republicans, however, vowed to continue the fight, and promised to chip away the funding of various aspects of the new health care law.

Most, if not all, of the court challenges come from different states whose attorneys general maintain that it is unconstitutional to mandate a citizen to purchase health care insurance. It is interesting to note that most of the attorneys general are appointed by Republican governors. There have been a few courts that have upheld the health care law, though these courts are in the minority. Suffice to say, the legal aspects of the new law will in all probability be decided in the United States Supreme Court.

For now, the tone of the " replace and repeal" debates have been marked with civility. Reason must be exercised, as well as prudence. There will be discussions ahead, and there will be room for debate. In the meantime, let us keep working on helping the 40 million uninsured Americans.

*Dave Brangan is a member of the South Carolina Association for the Advancement of Health Education and a health educator at the Orangeburg-Calhoun Free Medical Clinic. He can be reached by e-mail at **DaveB72@aol.com**.*

May 4, 2011

Healthcare Reform Does Not Mean Access to Care

The debate about House Bill 3962 is over. President Barack Obama has signed the papers, and now it is time to provide health care insurance to some 40 million Americans. For those who need immediate medical care, they will have to wait, as it will be at least three to four years before the forty million will be covered by a health care plan through Medicaid or some sort of health care exchange. But is the debate over, and now everyone goes home happy? Not by a long shot - and we would be hard-pressed to find a happy Republican!

Putting politics aside, health care reform does not mean access to care, or "getting in to see the doctor." Just ask anyone with Medicaid, and they will tell you that having Medicaid does not mean access to care. Some physicians do not accept Medicaid patients because it does not pay the physician very well. Medicaid is notorious for reimbursement that is too slow and too little. From a business viewpoint, the physicians are losing money. While I have never met a physician living at or below the federal poverty level, physicians have many support staff, nurses, receptionists and lab techs who very well may be. Therefore, many physicians do not accept Medicaid or Medicare patients at all, especially physicians who specialize in something other than primary care. Some physicians do accept Medicaid patients, and it is a discretionary decision. For Medicare patients - those who are 65 years of age and older or who might have a disability - the situation is quite similar, with poor and/or slow reimbursement rates.

These two programs must be adequately funded for health care reform to work. Budget cuts must come from somewhere if health care reform is to work. There are plenty of "out of control" government programs to choose from, but it must be done. As for health care exchanges, we will have to wait and see how they will work.

Money, however, is not always the problem. In case no one has noticed, there is a shortage of primary care physicians. These physicians are your family doctors, and they are, well, getting a little older. Physicians now graduating from medical school are joining large group practices or specializing in medicine rather than setting up a new practice to serve local communities. This problem needs to be addressed within health care reform, as well. One suggestion might be to train more nurse practitioners, who are able to see primary care patients for sore throats, ankle injuries and minor illnesses with back-up from an on-site physician. Another solution is the expansion of community health centers and free medical clinics, both of which have national and state infrastructures that could improve access to care for primary care patients. A community health center accepts Medicare, Medicaid, and uninsured patients. Those with no insurance must still pay a fee, typically $25 to $50. The balance is on a sliding scale based on income, and the patient is sent a monthly bill for the remainder of the cost. For now, free clinics do not charge anything to see a physician; however, they do not accept people with Medicaid and Medicare.

In summary, we can see that the health care system is quite complex with no guarantee that one will have access to care even if one has Medicaid or Medicare. And even if one has private insurance, there are deductibles to be met and co-pays on medication. Some deductibles can be as much as $1,000 on a family insurance plan.

While waiting for health care reform to become reality, one can always practice prevention, wellness, health education and proper nutrition. There seems to be renewed interest in these practices, which are growing in popularity thanks to Dr. Oz, Dr. Sonja Gupta and other physicians who appear on television daily.

May 4, 2011

Reform Not for Everyone

While the Patient Protection and Affordable Care Act of March 2010 is off to a good start, it is not for everyone. Obviously, if you have your own insurance plan - and it is a good one - you will keep it. The intent of the law is to provide coverage for some 40 million people (some estimates at 50 million) who have absolutely no insurance and use hospital emergency rooms for routine medical care, i.e., upset stomachs, sore throats, skin rashes, spider bites and so on. How about labor and delivery? If you have been following my articles, you have seen that about everyone who wants healthcare insurance will be covered. Please hold this thought as this article continues, as we will return to it later.

Hispanics who are not U.S. citizens are not covered by the new law. This opens a Pandora's box as to who is and who is not a legal resident of the United States. I am sure the U.S. Department of Immigration Services can help us identify who is and who is not a legal resident. In the meantime, there are gray areas, green cards, temporary visas, work cards and babies born in the U.S. My point is if we are going to have health care for all, let us have health care for all. Let us not say health care for everyone except Hispanics who are not U.S. citizens or undocumented workers. Of the 40 million people who are uninsured, several million are Hispanics.

Another segment of the American population that may be left out is the American Indian. They are exempt for mandatory participation when this aspect of the law begins in 2014. Despite my 35 years of working in public health, I am uncertain of the rationale of this part of the law. The Indian Health Service (U.S. Public Health Service) serves this population, which is situated in Midwest and Western states. These would be the traditional Indian reservations and recognized tribes. There are, however, Native Americans right here in North and South Carolina. Hopefully, this will not open another Pandora's box.

There is a third segment of the population that we have not talked about - yet. These are people who are not going to participate in the program. In other words, they are going to opt out and pay the penalty, which may be cheaper than buying the insurance. They may do this even though they just might get a rather excellent rate from the state exchanges. These folks will be young people under the age of 40 who think they will live forever and never have an accident or get sick, or folks who don't want the government to tell them what to do.

For those younger than 40 years of age, I was there once and felt the same way. I used to paint houses during the summers when going to college, climbed on ladders and rooftops with no medical insurance. My father used to exclaim, "You don't have insurance!" but I thought I would live forever and never fall off a roof. I never did, but I was lucky.

For the folks who don't want the government telling them what to do, I can empathize with that - as do attorney generals from several states who plan to challenge this aspect of the law in the courts. We will have to wait and see how this plays out. The problem is, we need participation - financial participation, which is - from these folks and the young folks to help pay for the total health care reform bill. If the courts find that it is illegal to require participation in the health care reform, then the money will have to come from somewhere else. Let us not throw out the baby with the bath water!

For the record, there are other groups of people who are exempt from participation in the health care reform law. They are active duty and retired military, veterans who use the Veterans Administration health care system, prisoners, religious objectors, and those who have low incomes. The low-income definition would be if the insurance premium would be more than 8 percent of a person's income.

Going back to "holding the thought" from the first paragraph, we can see not everyone who wants to have health care insurance will have it. The Hispanics who are not citizens and Native Americans will not formally be part of the health care reform insurance program. And many of those who will be eligible may not want it. How will they need to be persuaded to participate?

There is still time to work out the inequities of the bill - but not very much time. The November elections are right around the corner for many states, and the Republicans are gaining strength. President Barack Obama will have two more years before the general election in 2012 to make the health care reform law fair and equitable for all. This can be accomplished through incentives, tax credits, waivers, and some plain common sense.

May 18, 2010

The Journey Begins -

As promised, the various aspects of health care reform will be explained in this column. This information comes not from an expert in this field, but from the viewpoint of someone who has worked on the "front lines" in the health care system for more than 20 years. The front lines have been in public health departments, community health centers, free medical clinics, and health service organizations. Therefore, the viewpoint is that intersection between the health care system and the patient.

First up is health care reform for young people, ages 19 to 26 years of age. If you recall, children up to age of 18 who are living at or below the federal poverty level are eligible for coverage under CHIP, or the Children's Health Insurance Program. At age 19, they are too old and no longer eligible for CHIP.

Beginning in September, under the new health care reform bill, children ages 19 to 26 may be covered under their parent's private insurance plan. They will not have to go out and purchase their own. This is a good provision of the law. Young people at this age are just beginning their careers and are not making large salaries, not to mention the unemployment rate. In addition, the children or young adults do not have to be dependents (as defined by federal tax definitions), can be married and can be working for an employer who offers medical insurance.

There is room for flexibility with this provision of the law. Previously, the only way a dependent could stay on a parent's medical insurance is to be a full-time college student up to the age of twenty-three. Under the new provision, it does not matter whether a dependent is enrolled in college or not - he or she is still eligible.

So far, so good. However, let us re-examine the language of this provision. The provision says it is for dependents of a parent's private insurance plan. What about federal, state, and military insurance programs? If a parent has a federal, state, or military insurance program, are their dependents excluded? Active and retired military members use Tricare insurance, which was not covered in this legislation. Now, members of the House and Senate must scramble to get a bill passed to include members of the armed forces for this particular provision.

A second major problem is an obvious one. During the entire health care reform debate, the figure 40 million was used to describe the number of people without health insurance. Does this figure include dependents? It is difficult to say for sure, but I think not. If 40 million adults are without health insurance, then their dependents are without health insurance, too, even with the new health care provision. Shouldn't the priority be to get the 40 million adults health insurance first and then the dependents?

Even with these two shortcomings, this provision in the health care bill is a good one and a step in the right direction. It is the beginning of a journey that will be fraught with interpretations, shortcomings, omissions, inequities and, in some instances, confusion. There will be occasions when the law must be interpreted by a regulatory agency. However, it is important to go forward until universal health care is achieved.

*Dave Brangan is a member of the South Carolina Association for the Advancement of Health Education and a health educator at the Orangeburg-Calhoun Free Medical Clinic. He can be reached by e-mail at **DaveB72@aol.com**.*

Update on The Affordable Care Act 2024

Health and Wellness

    The Affordable Care Act was presented by President Barack Obama and passed by the United States Congress to help people without healthcare insurance in 2010. At this point, it is not necessary to delineate all aspects of the Affordable Care Act as that would be a book within itself. For now, we will discuss the Health and Wellness section which includes clinic-based health education. The National Prevention Health Promotion and Public Health Council was established by law. The law includes an array of health services to include preventive services such as mammograms for women (cancer prevention), immunizations, well visit checkups for Medicare recipients, and a host of other prevention serves. There were funds for hospitals, state health departments, community health centers and other designated healthcare organizations. There was some money for community-based organizations, but not very much. Before we look at facts and dollar figures, it is important to understand how funds are allocated and how they are distributed. While I am not an expert on grants and who gets what, I will attempt to give the reader an overview of Federal dollars in the form of grants. When Congress announces a major grant such as money for the National Prevention, Health Promotion and Public Health Council, a certain amount of money is allocated by Congress specifically for that purpose. Some grants are for research projects, and these are usually obtained by major colleges, universities, and research centers. The grant from the National, Health Promotion and Public Health Council is for practical applications for health programs in organizations such as the Centers for Disease Control and Prevention (CDC) in Atlanta Georgia and the National Institutes of Health (NIH) in Washington, DC. The NIH tends to be more research oriented whereas the Centers for Disease Control is more application oriented. The funds or money would go to the Centers for Disease Control to the State Health Departments. High population states such as New York and California would get more grant money compared to Idaho or North Dakota, for example, based on a high population. The States then make grant announcements for hospitals, community-based organizations, and other intermediary organizations, such as the Central Carolina Community Foundation, which makes further grants available to smaller organizations. This all sounds good on paper, until the money runs out or there is very little money left over for those smaller organizations which are low budget organizations such as non-profits. Back in the day, this was called the "trickle down affect" and there was not much money left after all the salaries and administrative costs were taken out of the original grant amount. Grants are very competitive, and it would not be unusual to have over 100 non-profits or more competing for a small grant offered from the State Health Department. The large healthcare organizations have the advantage of obtaining federal funding and if one knows a politician to help with the funding, that is even better. Having said all of this, I am a firm believer of local organizations pulling themselves up "by the bootstraps" to solve their own problems, especially when confronted with chronic diseases. Churches, schools, and other community based non-profit charitable organizations have been known to do this. There is no need to rely on the government, whether Federal or State or improve one's health. Some churches have really taken the initiative to have their own diabetes, hypertension and exercise classes on their own. It is not difficult. Lay health educators are becoming popular. For the most part, grants are "seed" money, in other words, enough money get started however it may not be enough for professional salaries, office equipment including computer and travel expenses. When the money runs out, health education, whether clinic based or community, will be over unless local funds are found. Local funds could be corporations, mini-grants, and if that does not work, it is back to fund raising for non-profits. Grants have a life cycle and a completion date. For the State of South Carolina, grants from the National Prevention, Health Promotion and Public Health Council grants were announced in 2011 to local organizations in the form of Request for Proposals (RFP). The funding awards were announced to a variety of health organizations and that was that. To my knowledge no funds were awarded to any of the South Carolina Free Medical Clinics. A final thought on Nation Prevention, Health Promotion and Public Health Council is that very little money was allocated for clinic-based patient education. This is where the "rubber meets the road" between healthcare providers and the patient. From here, I will present excerpts from the National Prevention, Health Promotion and Public Health Council which pertain to Health Promotion and Education to include clinic-based education. I want to emphasize that this is a well thought out document, contains wonderful information and adds value to the Affordable Care Act. I just wonder if it is enough where the "rubber meets the road." This will be preceded by my article in the Orangeburg, SC newspaper in 2010.

Appendix Five –

For the Academics - Excerpts from the National Prevention Strategy Affordable Care Act 2010

National Prevention Strategy Prevention lowers health care costs

- A proven program that prevents diabetes may save costs within three years.
- One of every five U.S. health care dollars is spent on caring for people with diagnosed diabetes.
- People who increased physical activity (2½ hours a week) and had 5 to 7 percent weight loss reduced their risk of developing type 2 diabetes by 58 percent regardless of race, ethnicity, or gender.
- A five percent reduction in the prevalence of hypertension would save $25 billion in 5 years.
- Annual health care costs are $2,000 higher for smokers, $1,400 higher for people who are obese, and $6,600 higher for those who have diabetes than for nonsmokers, people who are not obese, or people who do not have diabetes.
- A one percent reduction in weight, blood pressure, glucose, and cholesterol risk factors would save $83 to $103 annually in medical costs per person.
- Increasing use of preventive services, including tobacco cessation screening, alcohol abuse screening and aspirin use, to 90 percent of the recommended levels could save $3.7 billion annually in medical costs.326
- Medical costs are reduced by approximately $3.27 for every dollar spent on workplace wellness programs, according to a recent study.
- Dietary sodium is linked to increased prevalence of hypertension, a primary risk factor for cardiovascular and renal diseases. Cardiovascular disease alone accounts for nearly 20 percent of medical expenditures and 30 percent of Medicare expenditures.
- Reducing average population sodium intake to 2,300 milligrams per day could save $18 billion in health care costs annually.329
- Tobacco use accounts for 11 percent of Medicaid costs and nearly 10 percent of Medicare costs.330 • Tobacco screening is estimated to result in lifetime savings of $9,800 per person.331 Prevention increases productivity
- Indirect costs to employers of employees' poor health—lower productivity, higher rates of disability, higher rates of injury, and more workers' compensation claims—can be two to three times the costs of direct medical expenses.
- Workers with diabetes average two more workdays absent per year than workers without diabetes.
- Absenteeism costs are reduced by approximately $2.73 for every dollar spent on workplace wellness programs, according to a recent study.

Health Education Consultants Volunteers and Students

Kalvin Cobaris USC Practicum Student 2019

Alison Ernest and Nick Couchell, USC Students

USC Student, Robert Tyler, presenting Columbia Free Medical Clinic 2014

Megan Jones, USC Practicum Student 2021

Madison Naulty, USC Practicum 2022

Health Ed Volunteer at Spanish Health Fair

Santa's Helper Christmas Fundraiser 2014

Dave's Backyard Bar-b-q Summer 2017

Runners at Dreher Island 5-K Run 2018

Conner Lentz at Harbison Community Center

161

Nick Doyle USC Student Practicum 2021

Wildred Cook - Newberry Patient 2015

Marie Callahan at Irmo Okra Strut 2018

Marie Callahan, Peggy Ondrea & Karen Brangan

Akash Patel - USC Student Practicum 2022

Adam Gause - USC Student Practicum 2015

162

Health Ed Volunteers at Christmas Fundraiser

Kristi Coleman, Practicum Student, 2017

Dr. Corey Hunt, Medical Director, Newberry Free Med Clinic

Rafael Garcia, patient at Good Samaritan Clinic, bids you farewell and thanks for reading Dave's book!

Contact Information:

Health Education Consultants, Inc.

PO Box 308

Irmo, South Carolina 29063

Phone: 803-727-8837

Email: Healthedconsults@aol.com

On **Facebook** under:

Health Education Consultants Inc

Our **website**:

www.healthypeoplesc.com

Made in the USA
Monee, IL
14 December 2024

0568a0d4-b80f-4c4a-b394-e5d8aa2d5930R01